BAD BEHA
TANTRUMS AN

Dr John Pearce

BAD BEHAVIOUR, TANTRUMS AND TEMPERS

*Tried and tested ways of helping your
child cope with strong emotions*

Thorsons
An Imprint of HarperCollinsPublishers

Thorsons
An Imprint of HarperCollins*Publishers*
77-85 Fulham Palace Road,
Hammersmith, London W6 8JB
1160 Battery Street,
San Francisco, California 94111-1213

First published by Thorsons in two volumes as
Tantrums and Tempers and *Bad Behaviour*, 1989

1 3 5 7 9 10 8 6 4 2

© John Pearce 1993

John Pearce asserts the moral right to
be identified as the author of this work

A catalogue record for this book
is available from the British Library

ISBN 0 7225 2818 3

Phototypeset by Harper Phototypesetters Limited,
Northampton, England
Printed in Great Britain by
HarperCollinsManufacturing Glasgow

To Mary, Rachel, Clare and Anna

Contents

· · · · ·

7 Special Techniques

8 Questions and Answers

Introduction
· · · · ·

It is easy enough to become a parent. Keeping to all the good intentions that you started out with is another thing all together. It doesn't take long to discover that it is impossible to get it right all the time and that bringing up children is the biggest challenge and the greatest responsibility that there could ever be.

Unfortunately, part of a normal child's development is to be difficult, disobedient, to have tempers and at times to be generally bloody-minded – at least from a parent's point of view. Although knowing that it is normal for children to be little terrors at times may not be very reassuring, it does mean that your child is not the only one to behave badly and cause concern.

The aim of this book is to help you to work out for yourself what approach is likely to be the most effective when dealing with a difficult behaviour and angry moods. The ideas and the methods that I have outlined here should make it easier to avoid one of the most common causes of parental disagreement and argument: how best to react to your children's problem behaviour.

All the most common behaviour problems are covered in the book. There are practical guidelines that will help you to work out effective ways of encouraging your child to be better behaved. But this book is not particularly about difficult or disturbed children. It is about normal children and everyday problems which are not a major concern but that nevertheless take up your time and energy and could become much larger problems if allowed to continue.

Many of the tantrums and the bad behaviour that occur later on in adolescence or early adult life can be traced back to childhood.

It is all too easy for antisocial behaviour to be repeated over and over again until it becomes a fixed habit that is very difficult to change. It makes sense to deal with these problems when they first appear rather than take the easy way out and hope that they will just fade away on their own. Yes, most will improve with time, but to do nothing and hope for the best is taking a big risk.

Young children need a great deal of firmness and clarity in the limits that are set for their behaviour. They can only gain self-control by having control given to them from outside in the first place. Firm guidelines and a clear structure to everyday life will help your child to feel secure. And as the child grows older and has more self-control, you can gradually allow more freedom. It is often easier to give in to a child's unreasonable demands than saying 'no' and sticking to it. But being firm and definite about what you think is right is one way of showing your love and care for your child.

I would like you to feel that I am talking directly to you as you read through the book. If you don't agree with what I am saying or if you don't understand, read on and it should become clear why I have taken a certain line rather than any other. Don't hold back from having an argument with me in your imagination or asking others what they think. In this way you will become much clearer about what you believe yourself. If you are sure that you are right and your child is coping well with life, then all is well. If, on the other hand, you are unsure about how to deal with a particular problem, I would like you to follow my suggestions as closely as possible in spite of any reservations you might have. I have been very careful to give guidelines and advice only where I am confident that they are safe, reasonable and effective.

If you have followed the guidelines and they have not worked, please don't think immediately that I (or you) have got it all wrong. It is perhaps just that you are not sticking closely enough to the guidelines offered. So read them again, have another go and don't give up!

1
. . . . .

Understanding Discipline

It is a shame that the word discipline is often used in a negative and authoritarian way. The word comes from the Latin - *disciplina* - meaning teaching, which is both positive and constructive. Unfortunately, many people think of discipline as meaning punishment and being very strict, so they try and avoid using the word. Although there is no proof, it does seem as though the less people talk about discipline the more badly behaved children become and the more other possible causes are thought about, such as:

- food additives
- too much television
- both parents out working
- a breakdown of traditional values in society
- single parent families
- poverty and unemployment

In some individual cases there may be some evidence to support the causes listed above, but it would be wrong to generalize and say that nowadays all children are naughty and undisciplined. Indeed, a few children are very well behaved. Nevertheless there are many pressures in our everyday life that make it difficult to provide the time and care that children need, but don't feel despondent, there is a lot that you can do to make sure that your child is reasonably obedient and isn't a pain in the neck.

The poor outlook for difficult and disobedient children means that it is no good sitting around hoping that they will grow out of it – many of them won't. In fact, the longer a child goes on misbehaving, the longer the problems are likely to persist in the future. Most naughty children under the age of 5 grow out of it and become reasonably well behaved, but badly behaved children over 5 years old have a strong tendency to continue being difficult, disobedient and possibly delinquent. So, if you would like your child to be reasonably well behaved, you will have to start your discipline early on!

SPOILING

If babies and young children were reasonable creatures who understood that other people have needs as well, there would not be much of a problem. You could respond to their every need and they would stop being difficult and demanding just as soon as their needs were satisfied. Unfortunately babies are not born reasonable and they have to be taught that other people have needs too. Until children have learnt this lesson they tend to work on the principle of 'the more you get, the more you want'.

You can see that if you continue to give in to every want, you will end up with a child who is very demanding and doesn't take other people's needs into consideration, in short, a spoilt brat. You might imagine that it would be nice to be spoilt, but in reality it leads to a great deal of distress for the spoilt child, not to mention the parents. Why else do you think spoilt children whine, moan and cry so much? This is an important point, because it means that at some stage parents will have to stop satisfying their child's every need if they want to avoid their baby growing up into a spoilt young person.

SAYING 'NO'

Looking after a new baby is so exciting and time-consuming that it takes most parents ages before they realize that they should be saying 'no' sometimes. Many parents leave it until the child's demands have become excessive and difficult (if not impossible) to meet. For some parents this stage will be after a few months, but for other parents it may take several years before they realize that they have a little monster who is impossible to satisfy. By this time the child will be so skilled at being demanding and manipulative that it won't be easy to change things without a lot of hard work and some distress for everyone concerned.

Perhaps the best time to start saying 'no' is as soon as you feel that your child is being unreasonable. But how can you tell what is unreasonable? Here are some ideas to help you:

- the baby stops crying as soon as you pick it up
- the crying is not that of an ill child, and there are no other signs of illness
- the baby always cries at the same time of day (or night)
- giving any attention at all immediately stops the difficult behaviour
- the crying or problem behaviour starts again as soon as your attention is withdrawn, even though the child is well and has toys to play with.

You can see that even tiny babies can be unreasonable at times, so it is a good plan to start saying 'no' at a very early stage. In this way you can gradually introduce your child to the idea that there is a limit to how many needs can be met, and your child will gradually come to know the limits of what is acceptable and what is not. This is what discipline is all about.

It is worth while remembering that there are many ways of saying 'no', some of which are outlined below.

- with a sharp tone of voice
- giving a loud shout
- saying 'no' in a whisper
- shaking your finger

- frowning and making a cross face
- turning away and giving no attention.

SAYING 'YES'

You might think that all parents have to do is to be good at saying 'no' and their child will become well behaved, but this is not so. All that happens if you say 'no' frequently enough is that your child stops behaviour of any type and becomes inhibited. By being good at saying 'no' you will be able to stop much of your child's bad behaviour so at first it may seem as though you have a very good child. However, children also need to be told what they can do as well as what they are not allowed to do.

In theory it should be possible to say 'yes' and give praise every time a child does something good and as a result it would never be necessary to say 'no'. This is an interesting idea, but in practice it could never work because there are so many dangerous situations in our everyday life. The dangers of fire, water, electricity and roads have to be taught at an early age and it is much easier to say 'don't . . .' rather than 'do . . .'. However, it is very important to teach children about danger in a positive way as well as using negative words such as 'no' and 'don't'.

By using a positive approach to discipline and training, you will have much more effect on how your child copes with danger. However, discipline is not only necessary to protect a child from harm, it is also needed for the child to fit in and to become a useful member of society.

LOVE AND INDULGENCE

We often think of love not just as a feeling of affection and caring, but also as an act of giving and self-sacrifice. Certainly this is what parents need to do for their children: they have to give up something of themselves if the love that they have for their child is to have any lasting effect. Loving and giving are so closely related that parents sometimes show their love by being indulgent and giving in to their child's demands,s or by giving extra toys or food.

It is so much easier to be indulgent and to give toys and food, rather than giving up something of yourself, but children need your time and attention, your supervision and your protection – how difficult it is to be a parent! If you are too indulgent and give, for example, too many toys, your child will become more difficult and demanding. If on the other hand, you sacrifice your own needs too much, the child will become overdependent and family relationships will become tense and difficult. So indulgence has a negative and potentially harmful side as well as a positive, caring side, and parents have to keep the balance between being too indulgent and too self-sacrificing.

Here are some situations to watch out for, where it is especially easy to get the balance wrong and show your love for your child by being overindulgent or by giving up too many of your own needs.

- When your child is ill, it is necessary to be more loving and indulgent, but it can be overdone and it can be difficult to get back to normal when the child is better. In chronic or life-threatening illness it is particularly difficult to get the balance right.
- If one parent is rather strict, the other one will want to be more soft and indulgent to compensate for this.
- Youngest or only children, and of course first-born children, are often given extra love and attention which can easily involve indulgence or self-sacrifice.
- Divorced or separated parents will normally wish to show their children that they still love them in spite of all the sadness and distress that has occurred and this often takes the form of overindulgence.
- Parents who have had a deprived or difficult childhood are likely to give too much to their children because they have missed out themselves.

- Grandparents sometimes encourage parents to be overindulgent and give too much to their children.
- Some parents are soft and indulgent by nature and set themselves up to play the role of a martyr. If this is the case this role will be played in every aspect of the parents' life and not only when with their children.
- Parents who are ill or distressed will tend to give in easily, partly to make life easier, but partly because they feel guilty that they are not able to give enough of themselves to the child.
- Feelings of guilt are a common reason for parents being overindulgent and giving in easily. This happens quite frequently when parents have to spend extra time away from their children, for example, if they work full-time.

Most of us will recognize something familiar in these situations and this is why we all find it difficult to get the balance right; the balance between loving without overindulgence and caring without smothering.

STARTING AT THE BEGINNING

It doesn't take long for a new-born baby to do something that is unwanted and upsetting for the parents. It may only be crying when there is nothing obviously wrong or not taking the feed properly. At this young age we usually make allowances and think up all sorts of reasons why the baby might be difficult, such as:

- is it 'wind'?
- could she be teething?
- I think he must be hungry
- she might be overtired
- you can see he is in pain
- she doesn't like being alone
- he wants a cuddle

- she must be allergic to the milk
- he is just like his father, always making a noise!

It takes most parents quite a while to realize that sometimes their baby can be difficult for no more serious reason than that it is bored and wants to see some action. Even so, many parents do not see their baby as being unreasonable in its demands and they continue to make excuses for many years.

So when is it that children first become 'difficult' and start to manipulate other people in order to get their own way? Manipulation is often thought to be a sophisticated skill that only develops after several years' experience and a lot of practice. In fact it is a very basic and primitive ability and even very young babies quickly learn to become expert in it. A good example of manipulation is when a baby cries, but then stops immediately it is picked up, only to start crying again as spon as it is put down, and then to stop when picked up once more. This is what manipulation is all about and the baby soon has the parents trained to give a cuddle or at least some sort of attention just by crying. After a bit more practice at manipulation, it doesn't take long before the child learns that being difficult in other ways, apart from crying, can also produce results!

It may sound as though a baby lies in the cot, thinking to itself, 'I wonder how I can get some attention by being difficult'. It isn't quite like that. The baby, just like any other person, has certain needs which, if not met, will result in some degree of distress and discomfort. It is the discomfort that leads on to the difficult behaviour and parents are very quick to respond because they know that something must be wrong and that their baby is so small and helpless. However, it is just this rapid response from parents that teaches children that crying or being difficult produces results and brings rewards. So you can see that children learn from a very young age that crying and difficult behaviour are good ways of making their needs known and getting their parents to do something for them. Crying and being difficult are therefore *very* normal in young children!

AT WHAT STAGE DO CHILDREN KNOW RIGHT FROM WRONG?

It doesn't seem right to say that a crying baby is being naughty and this is why parents make all those excuses and allowances when children are young. Of course, it is important to do this - for a while. But sooner or later, unless your child is very unusual, it will become quite clear that unreasonable demands are being made.

Naughtiness is something which starts to develop during the first year of life and then becomes more obvious when children have learnt the difference between 'yes' and 'no'. You can see this when a baby crawls towards something dangerous like an electric socket, stops and looks at you, and then carries on in spite of hearing you say 'no'. At this early stage there is no feeling of guilt for wrongdoing and it would be inappropriate to describe the child as naughty because a clear understanding of right and wrong is only just starting to develop. It is not until about 3 years of age that children show obvious feelings of guilt, but a clear understanding of right and wrong and the rules of everyday life doesn't really develop until 7-9 years of age.

This is much later than most parents would think, but the gradual evolution of a child's understanding of what bad behaviour is must be taken into account when you decide whether your child is being naughty or not. In addition to your child's stage of development and understanding of right and wrong the following points should also be remembered when considering bad behaviour.

- Is the bad behaviour done on purpose or is it unintentional?
- Has the behaviour become an unconscious habit and therefore not deliberate?
- Does your child know for certain that the behaviour is unacceptable?
- Is the child just copying the bad behaviour of others in the family?

- Could the behaviour be a sign of illness or distress?
- Is the behaviour bad enough to discipline or is it best ignored?

There never seems to be enough time to work out the answers to these questions, but it is always helpful to sit down and think about these points, especially if a particular pattern of behaviour is frequently repeated or if you are not quite sure what to do about it.

SO WHAT IS BAD BEHAVIOUR?

In the end it is parents who have to decide where to draw the line between good and bad behaviour. This sounds easy enough, but in reality there are several questions that have to be sorted out first before a clear decision can be reached:

- Is the behaviour likely to harm or upset other people?
- Do the parents agree?
- Is the decision right for the child's stage of development?
- Is the decision in line with what the rest of society expects?
- Have the same standards been adopted for the rest of the family?
- Has the child been given a simple explanation of the decision?
- Will close relatives and friends support the parent's decision?
- Can the decision be kept by all concerned?

How do you decide what is right and wrong? This is more complicated than you might think because everyone has a slightly different idea about it, which is why in a court of law there is more than one person to make the decision. Obviously it is necessary for parents to agree on what is acceptable behaviour and on what limits will be set.

If parents can't agree with each other about where to draw the line, then it would not be surprising if the children were disobedient because they wouldn't know what was expected of them. Children need to have a very clear understanding of what exactly is required, otherwise they will make their own rules and do whatever they want. Even if parents agree and have clear rules of behaviour for the family, it is still possible for friends and relatives to undermine this by open disagreement or a disapproving attitude. Equally, if parents set standards of behaviour which are very different from those at school and in the rest of society then again children will become confused about what is expected of them.

Testing the limits of what is and is not allowed is a normal stage of development and it will mean that children will frequently be overstepping the mark and behaving badly. It is therefore quite unreasonable to get angry with children during this period of learning, which takes several years. It is also equally unreasonable to be too easy going and not to set clear standards of acceptance behaviour. If children are not given firm guidelines it will take an extra long time before they learn how far to go and when to stop.

LOVE AND DISCIPLINE

It may not be immediately obvious, but discipline and being strict can be a form of loving and caring. Children need to know what is right and wrong and need to have clear limits set on their behaviour. Discipline is about training and guiding children, and telling them exactly how far they can go. If you are able to be very consistent in limit-setting, your child will feel cared for and safe. However, this feeling of security will only occur if your limits are reasonable and fair for the stage of development that the child has reached. This is one of the many factors that make discipline so difficult: what is right at one age may be quite wrong at another. For example, allowing a 2-year-old to have a few tempers may not be unreasonable, but to let an older child indulge in tempers will only lead to more tantrums. Appropriate discipline and clear limit-setting is a way of protecting and loving your child. Without this special type of care your child will have great difficulty in coping with the rough and tumble of everyday life and will become unpleasant to be with.

Fair, firm and consistent discipline is, therefore, a way of showing your love for your child and, like other forms of love, it frequently involves giving and self-sacrifice. In order to be consistent, parents have to work hard to agree with each other and to apply the agreed standards, even when they are tired and fed up or would rather be doing something else. In the same way that parental love and care make children feel safe and happy, so good discipline helps children to feel secure and confident.

Your love will help your child feel happy, comfortable and good. Gradually this will help the child to develop self-confidence and a good self-image. In a very similar way, fair and consistent discipline will help your child to feel safe and secure, and eventually to develop self-discipline.

HOW CAN SELF-DISCIPLINE BE DEVELOPED?

The ultimate aim of teaching children about right and wrong, good and bad, is so that they can learn how to control and manage their own behaviour and make their own decisions about where to set the limits. Discipline, like all other forms of teaching, is a slow and sometimes painful business. It has to be repeated often and 'refresher courses' may be necessary from time to time. It is no good being angry if your child seems to be slow in learning. Most of us will remember how difficult it is to learn from a teacher who is cross and shouts at you, and how helpful it is when the teacher is clear and repeats things until you understand.

The close links between discipline and teaching are seen in the way both schools and parents have in recent years tended to encourage children to learn for themselves from an early age. It is now known that this system only works if a child has already been taught a reasonable level of self-discipline and self-control, and for most children this isn't before the age of 7–8 years. Nursery schools that only offer free play and lack a firm structure and control of the children are not helping with self-discipline – they may even be undermining what you are doing at home.

Children are not born with self-control and it will not develop unless you give firm and loving discipline in the early years. This is not at all easy because a necessary part of teaching is to allow your child the freedom to make mistakes. During the learning process children have to go from a state of high supervision and external control to very little, if their own inner control is to mature. It is a bit of a balancing act and here are some of the things that can go wrong:

- Children have very different personalities and some need firmer discipline than others.
- Some children are slow in their development and learning ability. They will require a high level of supervision and consistent limit-setting for much longer than usual.
- If your discipline is too tough and controlling, your child is likely to become too self-controlled and inhibited.
- Giving a high level of supervision and control for too long will lead to a child who is dependent and lacks self-confidence.
- Children who haven't had enough discipline when they were young usually lack self-control and cause unhappiness to themselves and others.

One way of looking at the task of teaching a child self-discipline is that it is a bit like learning to drive a car. You need a lot of supervision in the early stages and if your instructor doesn't have good control of the car you could easily have an accident. However, if the instructor does all the driving, you may never learn!

CONCLUSION

After all this it may seem as though being a parent and getting discipline just right for your child is virtually impossible. You're right, it is! So it is a good idea to be reasonably relaxed about any mistake you may make. Try and keep a sense of humour and realize that your child can learn from your mistakes as well!

2
. . . . .

Understanding Tantrums and Tempers

Tempers and tantrums are difficult to ignore, unsettle everyday life, are unpleasant to watch and may even be dangerous. Most of us would be happy if our children only occasionally became angry, rarely had a temper and never had a tantrum. However, it is important to remember that it is quite normal for young children to go through a phase of having tantrums. There could even be some cause for concern if your child doesn't show signs of anger as he or she grows older.

Children vary a lot in the ways they show their anger, depending on many different factors. These can include:

- the child's temperament
- family expectations
- the child's sex
- cultural background
- the child's age and stage of development
- family communication
- the child's physical and emotional state
- social factors

The various causes of tempers work together a bit like watercolour paints: you start with red and yellow, mix the two together and you have three different colours – red, yellow and orange. Add a third colour, like blue, and you have a whole range of colours. This is called an 'Interactive Relationship' where the interaction of individual factors produces more causes than the separate factors alone.

Although each of the main groups of causes is mentioned separately here, it is important to remember that they all react with each other in this complicated way. If you want to know *why* your child has a bad temper, you should be able to work it out from what follows, but don't look for a *single* cause. It might help to make a list of every factor you can think of and then give each one a 'contribution' score from 0-10 so that in the end you will have a better idea about what is causing your child's tempers, if there is a pattern to them, and what you might be able to change. You could also get another adult who knows your child well to do the same and then compare results.

TEMPERS AND TEMPERAMENT: THE DIFFICULT CHILD

'Temperament' is used to refer to the way a child will generally react to situations and to the usual way it behaves and shows emotions. The temperamental characteristics combine to form the personality, which gradually becomes more clearly formed as the child grows older. Even at birth, though, children have different temperaments and, in fact, there is evidence that a large part (maybe as much as 80 per cent) of our temperament is inherited. You only have to look at new-born babies in the nursery to realize how different they are from each other.

At birth some babies are placid, easy and predictable in their behaviour, while others are restless, difficult and unpredictable. Often it is possible to recognize the temperament of a baby even before birth, by its activity level and responsiveness to what is happening to the mother. Differences in behaviour and emotions are therefore largely 'constitutional', that is, how the person is made. This does not mean that what happens in the child's environment is not important – quite the opposite. It is the finishing touches that make all the difference.

One way of looking at personality is to think of it as being rather like a picture. A child is born with a certain type and size of canvas, brushes and a unique personal set of colours, which, to some extent, will decide the make-up of the child's personality. In the end it is the person's life experiences that will make up the final picture, although this will be limited by what they started out with.

It is increasingly recognized that some babies are born difficult. The so-called 'Difficult Child' is easy to recognize because he or she has the following characteristics right from the start:

- unpredictable – usually difficult to feed, to put to bed or to toilet and then sometimes easy
- very strong emotions – usually having tempers and crying, rather than being happy
- easily disturbed by change – slow to settle and difficult to comfort.

If you happen to have a child with a difficult temperament you will immediately recognize these characteristics. You have a tough time ahead of you but don't despair. There are things that you can do to help your child and many children will have grown out of it before they start school. Of course, lots of children would fit into the description given above, but it is possible to distinguish between children who are *born* with a difficult temperament and behave in this way right from the start and other children who have been allowed to *learn* how to get attention and get their own way by being difficult.

Children who have a difficult temperament that is present from birth have a much higher rate of problem behaviour and tempers than easygoing children. They are also more likely than other children to have cuts that require stitching, which is just one sign of how serious the problems really are! Children with a difficult temperament also require 'extra super' parenting if they are to be helped, so it is not going to be easy. They need more of the following than you would normally provide:

26

- routine and regularity
- clear limit setting
- high level of supervision
- firm, consistent discipline
- frequent comfort and reward.

If you are able to provide this extra care, most children will learn to modify their temperament reasonably well by the time they start school, but some children will continue to be difficult and then it is just a case of carrying on with the guidelines above with determination and increased intensity.

The guidelines above should be helpful for any difficult child, but you will have noticed that there is a strong emphasis on regularity, consistency and firmness. This is hard work for anyone and it will also be hard for your child. If you have decided that your child needs this type of help, it is most important to balance the rather controlling form of care with a great deal of positive care and love. Otherwise you will find that you are forever getting at your child and saying things like, 'stop it', 'be quiet', 'come here', 'don't . . .'!

You may find it difficult to be loving towards a child who has lots of tempers and is frequently irritable and disobedient, so you have to work at it. Here are some ways of balancing all the negative experiences that your child will go through if he or she has a difficult temperament.

- Try and avoid situations that you know your child is going to be unable to cope with without being very difficult and temperamental. These occasions only give your child practice in how to be difficult and annoying! However, if it is something like getting dressed in the morning or going to the toilet, you obviously can't avoid it. In this case a regular routine is helpful, so that your child becomes used to doing things automatically, and knows that arguments and tempers are pointless.

- Look out for any good thing that your child does, especially if he or she manages to control temper in a satisfactory way and give lots, tons, gallons, heaps, oodles of praise. Don't worry about going over the top with your praise, it is difficult to give too much.
- Set up situations that you know your children should be able to cope with without losing their tempers even though they may not get their own way. This gives them practice in temper management and gives you a time to give praise rather than telling them off again.
- Arrange special times when your child is alone with you or another adult, purely to enjoy the time together. This is 'high quality time' and many times more worthwhile than being together in the ordinary way, when you have something else to do at the same time, for example the cleaning or making a meal.

Many parents use 'high quality time' without really knowing what they are doing – it just seems the natural thing to do. With a difficult child, though, you have to think things out and work hard at it for it to have any effect. Here are some guidelines for getting the best from this special time:

- do something that you both enjoy, such as a game, playing outside, going for a walk, or just talking
- make sure that there are no distractions (like the TV) or disturbances (such as other people coming into the room)
- it is best to keep this special time short and intensive so that you both finish feeling that you would like to do it again – five minutes of high quality time every day or every few days may be quite sufficient and better than many hours of ordinary time.

This special time reminds children that they are indeed special themselves and that what they do is important to you. In other words you are showing that you care for your child and love him or her, even if you have to be firm and tough at times.

TEMPERS AND TEMPERAMENT: THE EASY CHILD

Some children are amazingly easy to bring up and rarely, if ever, have a temper or tantrum. Although this could be due to your being a wonderful parent it may also be that you have a child with an easy personality who has none of the characteristics of the difficult temperament. But there are other possible reasons for a child not having much of a temper, such as:

- an anxious and sensitive child will tend to avoid getting angry, because it is too upsetting. This child needs to learn how to be angry without it getting out of control. It might be a good idea to have a joke about how to be angry and get the child to practise being cross
- some children who are very slow and backward in their development are rather quiet and passive. If this is the case, the delay in development will become more obvious as the child grows older. There are lots of things that can be done to improve their skills but not much that will change their ability level
- if you are a very strict and restrictive parent, your child will not dare to show his or her temper (but may do so when you are not present). It is worth thinking about this possibility if you get reports of your child having lots of tempers when away from you, but when at home he or she behaves perfectly
- it could be that you are too easygoing and indulgent. If you give in to every wish of your child it is possible to avoid tempers and tantrums for quite a long time . . . but not forever!
- perhaps you have done a good job and helped your child to manage his or her temper very well!

FAMILY EXPECTATIONS

Parents have certain expectations of how their child should behave and any parent would be happy if these expectations were met all the time. Life is much more complicated than this, because children often have other ideas and so do other relatives and friends. However, the standard of behaviour that parents set is important in guiding the child to understand what is acceptable and what is not.

There are a number of influences that affect the way parents develop their own expectations of acceptable behaviour and it is useful to know what they might be:

- there is a very strong tendency to repeat your own childhood experiences of parenting with your child
- if your parents were either too strict or too soft with you, you will have a tendency to counteract this and go too much in the opposite direction with your own child
- if you think your partner is too strict or too soft, this will also make you likely to counterbalance this and swing too much the other way
- the religious, social, political and national culture you have adopted will probably affect you more than you would care to admit
- your own personality will obviously play a part in what you are prepared to put up with
- your age will also make a difference: young parents tend to be rather too soft and easygoing and elderly parents usually have high expectations of good behaviour
- parents probably have higher expectations of their first child and lower standards for their youngest child
- most parents also have different expectations for their daughters and their sons: on the whole, boys are able to get away with more aggression and tempers than girls - yes, even these days!

It is remarkable that children (and even teenagers) tend to follow their parents' wishes and opinions on most major issues, provided that the parents' views are clear and consistent. Where this is not so, the children are more likely to 'do their own thing'. If both parents can agree on what they expect from their children and they make this very clear, then the children will know exactly where they are and eventually most of them will fit in and conform.

These family expectations take a while to build up and develop into a 'family tradition', but this can become a very strong and influential force, particularly if the family is a large one. Equally this influence of the family can be undermined by grandparents or other family members who have other ideas.

Building up a family tradition is an effective way of getting your child to behave and conform, without having to say too much yourself. If your family tends to argue and show aggression, don't be surprised if the children do the same, they are only conforming and keeping to the family tradition!

Ask yourself, 'What expectations and traditions have I got in my family?' If you are not sure, then this will also be the case for your child and you might be better off if you established some. It will need a lot of careful discussion and thought. Don't be put off if you are on your own or if your partner is uncooperative - in some families it is left to one parent only to decide these issues, and this can be successful even if it is much harder work.

These expectations and traditions lead to the family developing its own style or way of coping. Some families will show little anger, while others may accept anger and tempers as a normal way of getting what you want. There is little evidence that either approach is better than the other and, provided there is consistency and agreement between the parents, it would only be in extreme cases that there might be a problem.

DO BOYS HAVE MORE TEMPERS THAN GIRLS?

Yes, boys do indeed have more tempers than girls. They are also more aggressive and show more anger. This certainly fits with what most people would expect, which in itself may be the main reason for this difference. In other words there are different standards of behaviour for the two sexes and boys live up to the expectation that they are more aggressive than girls. Generally parents, particularly fathers, play more rough and tumble, 'mock fights' with their sons and behave differently towards them from an early age.

The difference between boys and girls tends to increase as they become older. This could be due to increasing social pressures to behave in an aggressive way or there could be other influences at work. Although baby boys and baby girls may appear much the same in their behaviour at birth, boys are more vulnerable or 'at risk' than girls right from the start:

- there are many more miscarriages of male than female foetuses
- at birth there is a difference of about a week in maturity with boys being more delayed
- this immaturity of boys continues and increases so that by eight years of age there is a difference of a year that increases to two years by puberty (males never catch up – at the other end of life there is still a difference and females live five years longer than males)
- more boys are born with some form of handicap than girls
- more boys die in the few weeks before and after birth, but, to 'compensate' for this, more boys than girls are born
- all developmental problems such as bed-wetting, soiling, speech and language difficulty, clumsiness, reading and spelling problems and hyperactivity, are all more common in boys
- boys have a higher rate of psychiatric problems than girls, even though in adult life it is females who suffer more frequently.

It would be impossible to explain these differences purely in terms of social influences and it is clear that there are strong biological or constitutional factors that make boys more vulnerable than girls. It is likely to be this biological immaturity, as well as the effect of social attitudes, that leads to an increased frequency of tempers and aggression in younger boys.

Also, one possible explanation for this increased vulnerability in boys is that they have less chromosomal or genetic material than girls, since they are missing a leg of the X chromosome:

$$\text{Female} = XX \qquad \text{Male} = XY$$

It is thought that the female's extra genetic material has a protective and controlling influence on the other genes that is absent in boys. There is some suggestion that the Y chromosome itself may have an influence on aggression and tempers. This is because some research showed that people with one or more extra Y chromosomes were found to be more aggressive than normal. Recently, however, there has been some doubt about this.

There is another important biological influence in older boys. This is the effect of the hormone testosterone, which begins to increase its production about two years before there is any physical sign of puberty. It is well recognized that high levels of testosterone in either animals or humans lead to increased muscle power and a raised level of aggressive drive. It is interesting to note that testosterone also increases in girls at puberty, but the increase is much smaller than in boys.

In spite of these very real differences between boys and girls in the frequency of angry behaviour and tempers, which have both a social and a biological basis, most of the variations between individuals are caused by other influences and not just by being male or female.

CULTURAL INFLUENCES ON TEMPERS AND ANGER

Quite apart from the factors within the individual and the family that affect the way anger is dealt with, there are also wider influences that come from outside the family. Some Asian cultures have a strong tradition of not showing anger. For example, Burmese children are taught to smile and be pleasant even if they are feeling frustrated and angry. Sikh children are taught to be humble, which means controlling feelings of resentment and anger against others.

Not only are there differences between national cultures, but there are also variations within cultures from time to time, rather like a pendulum swinging. For example, the suppression of anger was seen as a desirable quality in Victorian times, but in the last 50 years or so in most Western cultures there has been an increasing move towards 'free expression' of feelings. This has had far-reaching effects on the standards by which children are brought up. However, it looks as if people in Britain think that the culture of free expression has gone far enough and they are now keen to push the pendulum back the other way a bit!

Religion plays an important part in many cultures in setting the moral standards by which families run their lives. The reduced influence of religion in many Western societies has resulted in a weakening of moral values. To some extent the State also sets standards with the 'laws of the land', but these laws are only applicable at the extremes of behaviour and hardly deal with the important issues of personal loyalty, honour, responsibility, relationships and caring. It is therefore not surprising that many parents are unclear about their own moral standards and that their children often have difficulty distinguishing right from wrong.

If your child asks you, 'Why is it wrong to have a temper tantrum?', ideally you should have an immediate answer that is convincing for you and seems right. Here are some possible answers:

- temper tantrums upset other people
- God does not like tantrums
- tantrums are unacceptable in our family
- grown-up people don't have tantrums
- tantrums make things worse for you
- it is wrong to force your will on other people
- people won't like you if you have tantrums
- tantrums will get you into trouble.

None of these answers are completely right or satisfactory. There are many other things that you could say, but it is important that you have thought about it and you have worked out your own values. If your child is not able to get standards of behaviour from you then he or she will get them from somewhere else which may not be so acceptable!

STAGES OF DEVELOPMENT

Very young babies cry, go red in the face and seem to be angry, but it is often not clear what all the fuss is about and, even later on, it is not unusual for a child to cry for no apparent reason. Gradually, as the child becomes more mature, the crying and the associated behaviour is more obviously a temper.

Tempers reach a peak frequency around two years of age and, in some ways, they are at their worst then. Hence, this stage is sometimes called 'the terrible twos', but the age of the child is not as important as the stage of development. If your child is immature or slow in development then the temper stage will be reached later and last longer.

At two years of age, about 20 per cent or one in five children have tempers that are regarded as a problem by their parents. At this stage two to three tempers a day lasting five to ten minutes, would be within the normal range and even an occasional temper lasting for longer is not necessarily abnormal at this age.

The reason for the frequent tempers around the age of two is related partly to problems that a two-year-old has in communicating, but another important reason is that two to three years of age is the time when children first become aware of themselves as individuals. They start referring to themselves as 'me' rather than by their name and later 'I' rather than 'me'. This increasing awareness of the Self is also seen when children recognize themselves in photographs without someone else pointing them out. Also, between two and three years of age, children looking in a mirror recognize themselves and, if they have a dirty mark on their face, they will rub it off their own face rather than rub the mirror. Thus, children at this stage of development become aware of their own identity and their individual needs.

By five years old, 10 per cent of this age group still have problem tempers but it would not be abnormal for a five-year-old child to have an occasional temper lasting 10 minutes or so and to have one to two tempers a day lasting for a few minutes only. At 10 years of age, many days should be free of tempers and any tempers that do occur should last only a few seconds, but may occasionally last up to five minutes.

As tempers become less frequent they also change in character. The violent first stage of the temper gradually gets shorter, but the sulking second stage grows longer, until adolescence, when tempers once again become more numerous and sulking and brooding is common.

Most two-year-olds have tempers that are caused by conflict with the parent when they are told that they must not do something. Arguments over toileting are also frequent, followed later by tempers over dressing. By five years old, many of the tempers are directed at other children and concern joint play. Of course these are generalizations and each individual child is different, but it will give you an idea about what most other children are doing.

FAMILY COMMUNICATION

Communication is a very important part of tempers, because tempers are a clear and sometimes dramatic way of letting people know that you are not getting what you want and you are distressed about it to the extent that you are prepared to upset others. For this reason it is very rare for tempers to occur in private. If you put a child with a temper tantrum in a room on its own, either the temper will stop or the child will increase the amount of noise it is making to be sure that you can hear. Occasionally children in a temper will do something really devious or destructive to make absolutely sure that your attention is focused on them.

Tempers occur most frequently at the stage of development (about two years old) when children have a good understanding of the meaning of many words (200 words at two year old), but still have some difficulty in putting the words together into sentences. As a result, communication can be frustrating for them and it is easy to misunderstand what they are trying to say.

Children with communication problems due to deafness, language problems or slow development are more likely to have tempers for the reasons outlined above. Partial deafness is very common in young children, and it is often associated with infections of the ear, nose and throat. It is easily missed and difficult to test for. If you are in doubt, it is best to get your child's hearing tested professionally and, if you are still doubtful, then ask to see a specialist.

Deafness owing to infections may vary from time to time, which can cause a lot of confusion. It may help to develop your own test, like whispering something your child would normally respond to, for example, 'It is time for bed' or 'Would you like an apple?' Or, you could use the tick of a clock or watch and move it slowly away from your child's ear and note the point at which the tick is no longer heard. Make sure that you cover the other ear while doing the test. When you have noticed the distance of the vanishing point of the tick you should then do the same test with somebody who has normal hearing and compare the two results. Both these tests can be easily made into a game and are good fun for children, but they will only give you a rough indication of your child's hearing.

Speech and language problems are associated with tempers and difficult behaviour. Speech problems include stammering and all forms of unclear speech, while language problems involve a more complicated disorder of the understanding and organization of words. Sometimes the disorder of language is very subtle and only affects one aspect, such as the expression of language where the child understands but can't find the right words to communicate with. Not surprisingly these children easily become frustrated and angry. As with most developmental delays these problems are more common in boys than in girls.

Parents may also have communication problems that can occur in several different forms:

- the 'Double Message' is a common problem of communication: the parent says one thing but seems to mean something else – for example, the instruction, 'Go to bed' is said with a tone of voice and a smile that says, 'I am not really serious about this' or, to give another example, 'I am not having any bloody swearing in this house'
- some parents are keen that their children should understand exactly *why* they have to do something and so give long and complicated explanations, but, unfortunately, many children stop listening after the first minute or so and they are left more confused than they were before
- inconsistent communication is a problem for all parents and is one of the most frequent causes of anger, resentment and tempers for both parents and their children – parents may say contradictory things at different times or in different places, they may also be inconsistent in what they say to different children, but the most disruptive form of inconsistency is when parents disagree between themselves and have different standards for their children's behaviour
- unclear speech is quite rare in adults, and children quickly learn what their parents mean if the words are given a strong emphasis and are accompanied by clear gestures
- deaf parents will obviously have difficulty in communication, but their children quickly learn to communicate and develop normal language themselves and, interestingly, deaf children of deaf parents often develop better communication skills than deaf children of normal-hearing parents

- parents whose mother tongue is different to that of their child may have problems in communicating with their child depending on what language is spoken at home and how proficient the parent is at speaking it, but, once again, much will depend on how good the parent is at using gestures and their tone of voice.

In addition to these problems there are other more subtle forms of family communication difficulties, for example:

- **'The Family Secret':** the parents have a secret that they wish to keep from other people, but their secretive and guilty behaviour alerts the children that something is not quite as it should be. The children may then imagine that something must be badly wrong and become emotionally unsettled, which, in turn, may lead to tempers
- **'The Stiff Upper Lip'** family who don't show their feelings and try and avoid people getting upset at any cost, will generally have children who also don't show when they are angry and, though all may seem to go well, angry feelings may come out in other ways (often as physical symptoms) or they may suddenly explode and give everyone a terrible shock
- **'The Family Myth':** although there are many possible myths, one that frequently affects tempers in children is the linking together of two family members because they are thought to be the same, for example, 'Johnny has his father's temper' or 'Jenny takes after her great-aunt Sally who was well known for her bad temper' – clearly this makes it difficult for the child *not* to have a temper!
- **'The Family Label':** here a child gets a label that is difficult to change even if the child wants to – 'The Angry One' or 'The Defiant One' will encourage the child to have tempers and be difficult
- **'The Family Style':** this is perhaps the most subtle form of communication of all and yet it is very influential. Each family

develops its own way of dealing with stressful situations and coping with anger and usually this is not spoken about, it just happens. Obviously it is the parents who set the tone and the children fit in and follow what their parents do - for example, some families argue a lot, talking in an aggressive way to each other and the children copy this style of communicating, which may work well within the family, but, outside the family, there are likely to be misunderstandings and the children will be thought to be aggressive by normal standards. Usually, neither the child nor the parent is aware of any problem because it is part of everyday life.

THE CHILD'S PHYSICAL AND EMOTIONAL STATE

Sick children tend to be more irritable and have more tempers. Parents compensate for this by being indulgent and giving in to their child's wishes to avoid any distress. It is important to do this while the child is unwell, but as the child gets better, it is sometimes difficult to change.

Obviously if your child is acutely ill, he or she will benefit from your care and indulgence, but at some stage you will have to return to normality otherwise your child might decide it is rather nice being spoilt and given into and find he can control you and get his own way by threatening to get upset and having a temper.

There are hardly any conditions where a short period of upset would be harmful for your child, provided that you are just doing what you would normally do. In fact, by being normal you will actually reassure your child that things are not too terrible. Or, put the other way round, the more you indulge a sick child the greater will be his anxiety that the illness is serious. Even if this should be true, it is helpful for seriously ill children to remain optimistic and as normal as possible, so they should be *treated* as normally as possible.

Tempers are more likely to occur when a child is hungry or tired.

You can therefore expect them before meals and later on in the day. A common time for irritability and tempers occurs when a child returns from the nursery or school because she will be both tired *and* hungry. Fortunately, both these problems are easily dealt with and it is a good idea to provide a snack and a quiet time as soon as your child returns home (it might also be effective for the parent who is irritable on arriving home from work!)

Children who are under emotional stress for any reason at all are more prone to irritability, tempers and aggression. Sometimes it can be difficult to tell that your child is under stress because children (and adults) tend to try and pretend that the stress isn't there in the hope that it will go away. Irritability and tempers that come out of the blue and are unexpected are therefore a useful sign that your child is experiencing stress and that she is having a problem coping.

SOCIAL FACTORS

We have seen how tempers and disruptive behaviour are associated with factors that relate to the child such as personality, age and sex and factors that arise within the family such as attitudes, communication and expectations. There are also more general social factors that are associated with tempers and behaviour problems as follows:

- living in the town or city is linked with an increased rate of tempers. The reason for this is unclear, but it is likely that there are many different stress factors that occur more often in areas of dense population – for example, poor housing, overcrowding, unemployment, broken homes and lack of play space
- lack of a father figure increases the risk of tempers, particularly in boys. This may be due to the fact that discipline is more of a problem for a single parent, or emotional disturbance following the loss of a father or identifying the child as being

difficult, 'just like his father' - the same being true, of course, if the father is the single parent but with the loss of the mother obviously being the cause of the disturbance

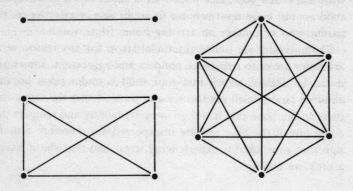

Possible arguments with different combinations of family members - the more family members, the more possibilities there are.

- large families seem to have more arguments, but you might expect this because a family of two can only argue with each other, a family of three has three combinations of people to argue with, a family of four has six chances and a family of six has 15 possible arguments they can have with different combinations of family members!
- mothers who smoke heavily are more likely to have a child with temper tantrums, but the reason for this is not clear. It could be that these are mothers who are under stress with many adverse circumstances to deal with, but there are many other possible explanations for the association between cigarette smoking and tempers
- children who live in the North and the Midlands are also supposed to be more likely to have tempers - goodness knows why!

CONCLUSION

Although a lot is known about tempers - when they occur, what causes them, who has them and so on - this is very general knowledge that has been gained from studying large groups of children. It is interesting and tells us something about the mechanisms of tempers, but it does not tell us about individual children - about your child. Each child is unique and if you want to know what causes your own child's temper you will have to work it out for yourself, taking into account all the factors that you can think of as I've outlined them above.

3
· · · · ·

Understanding Anger and Aggression

WHAT IS ANGER?

Anger, perhaps more than most emotions, is self-centered and selfish. It occurs when someone is unable to have what he wants, when he wants it. An angry emotion may also develop if a person feels there is a threat that he will not get his own way. So when a child is told that it can't have an ice-cream even though the ice-cream van is playing its jingle and other children are having ices, an angry scene often follows. The boy is angry and wants to have the ice-cream immediately. He won't be satisfied by being told that he can have one tomorrow. The parents, on the other hand, are angry as there is a threat that they may not get what they want, which is to have a reasonably obedient child. Anger is therefore strongly bound up with a person's ego or selfishness and is driven by a primitive and basic desire to have personal needs satisfied.

The word 'anger' comes from the Latin *angere*, meaning 'to strangle', which sounds pretty bad! But anger is more often used as a very general and broad term, which ranges from mild irritability at one end of the spectrum, to violent aggression at the other. Tempers are somewhere in the middle, with tantrums being further up the scale towards all out aggression. The word 'aggression' comes from the Latin *aggredi*, meaning 'to attack'. It implies that a person is prepared to force his own will on another person or object even if this means that physical or psychological damage might be caused as a result.

Compared with most other emotions, anger is a fairly simple and straightforward feeling, but it can combine with other moods to make up more complicated emotions such as jealousy or grief. For example, jealousy includes the following feelings: anxiety, anger, hate, fear, misery, hopelessness and frustration. It is unlikely that anger ever occurs entirely on its own as a single mood state. Anger is normally accompanied by anxiety, possibly because there is always a chance that the angry person's wishes will not be met and he won't get what he wants when he wants it. Certainly it is a common experience to feel very anxious when being angry. It can be a rather disconcerting experience to feel really angry but at the same time to feel so panicky, anxious and shaky that it is difficult to express the anger clearly.

THE LINK BETWEEN ANGER, AGGRESSION AND OTHER EMOTIONS

The association between anger and aggression is obviously a close one. What differences there are depend more on semantics than anything else. Most people would see aggression as a more extreme form of anger that has a strong physical component. But we also use the word aggression to describe the emotional drive that athletes have in order to do well, which does not involve much in the way of anger. However, there is a link between these two meanings of aggression, which is that both aim to put another person or competitor down in an inferior position.

Of all emotions it is anxiety that is the most commonly experienced. It is even more common than anger. There is a very close connection between anger and aggression and anxiety and it is important to understand the nature of this relationship. An emotional reaction occurs as a response to a stress, which may be caused by an event outside a person, such as being told you can't have an ice-cream, or by an event inside the person, such as the thought, 'I think my parents love my sister more than me'.

Whenever a stressful event occurs, the first feeling to be experienced is anxiety, which explains why it is the most frequently occurring emotion. If the stress is mild then there is unlikely to be any progression on to other emotions, but if the stress increases, sooner or later anger will develop. An example of this would be a child who is jealous of his sister and is under stress in situations where he could be treated unfairly. When he sees his mother get a bag of sweets out he becomes anxious that he won't have his fair share and watches carefully, anxiously counting out the sweets. If the sister is indeed given more sweets than him, his stress becomes greater and he may then become angry and aggressive. So, where there is anger you should expect to find anxiety as well. You will see this in yourself when you are angry – do you remember the anxious feeling, the shaking and the 'butterflies in the stomach' feeling that occur when you are angry?

The physical and psychological symptoms are much the same for anger as they are for anxiety, although they will tend to be rather more severe in states of anger and aggression. It can sometimes be very difficult to tell whether a child is angry or just very anxious, because the behaviour can be so similar. For example, a boy with school phobia will become increasingly anxious as he gets closer to school. Eventually he may develop quite aggressive behaviour in his attempts to avoid going to school, even though the reason for this is his worry about being able to cope in school.

If the stress continues to increase, the anger and anxiety will also increase until eventually a state of depression and misery may result. It is often the case that a temper will end in tears and, in our example of the jealous boy, he too may finally become withdrawn and feel miserable and unloved if he is continually made to feel jealous and angry. Once again the physical symptoms of anxiety and anger are also the same for depression and misery and you should always expect depression to be accompanied by both anger and anxiety.

THE DEVELOPMENT OF ANGER AND AGGRESSION

If a baby does not arrive in the world crying and making a lot of noise, we become worried, but it is very difficult to know exactly what emotion the baby really is experiencing. It could be anger and resentment at leaving the nice warm womb or it could be that being born is a very uncomfortable process that makes the baby cry in pain. It is not until a child is a few months old that it is possible to be sure that anger is the mood that is being expressed rather than a much less specific form of distress. Gradually, children become more able to express anger and get into a temper until during the second year they become very skilled at it! It is at this time that tempers reach the peak of frequency and the expression of anger is well developed, but yet to be controlled or 'tamed'.

Aggression deliberately directed against another person does not really show itself before the age of 18 months but becomes more obvious over the next few years. Tempers, on the other hand, actually tend to become shorter, but the effects of any violence become greater as the child becomes bigger and stronger. So aggression develops more slowly and reaches a fully developed stage (but not necessarily controlled) some time during adolescence. As the anger and tempers are brought more under control the time spent brooding and sulking usually gets longer, so it may seem as though the temper is going on for longer as the child grows older even if this is not really the case.

In the first two years, most of the anger and tempers arise as a result of conflict with parents - first over toileting and doing dangerous things and later over tidying away toys and dressing, but the precise nature of the tempers will vary from one child to another. By the age of five years a large number of arguments are with other children rather than with parents and the children frequently turn to aggression and fighting as a way of resolving disputes.

The socializing effects of school play a significant part in reducing the frequency of tempers. The child comes under the influence of other children and adults who don't make the same allowances for bad behaviour as may happen at home. From school age onwards, tempers are mostly confined to the home and involve those who are nearest and dearest.

CONCLUSION

Anger and aggression are very closely linked together and also with other emotions. The link with anxiety is a particularly close one. All emotions develop stage-by-stage as the child grows older and it is helpful to know something about this in order to be able to work out the best way to understand and cope with your child's tempers and tantrums.

48

4
. . . . .

Coping with Bad Behaviour

BEFORE YOU START

All children have their own unique way of being difficult and, because each is so varied, they will all require a type of discipline which is specially designed to meet their individual needs – what you might call 'designer discipline'! A lot of careful thought is necessary before you start to deal with bad behaviour. It is also necessary to take into account the circumstances in which the bad behaviour occurs. It isn't so much a case of a particular type of discipline being good or bad, it is more a question of what is best for your child in a given situation.

Before you start to discipline your child you should take into account the following four factors.

1. The child's personality

Sensitive children, who are easily upset, are usually very responsive to any kind of discipline and also to other people's moods. With this type of child it shouldn't be necessary to raise your voice much or even to be at all strict. If you are even a bit too cross, the sensitive child may become so upset that the point you were trying to correct gets lost and forgotten among the tears. On the other hand a tough, *thick-skinned* and rather insensitive child will require a very firm, clear and definite type of discipline. Any lack of clarity or indecision on the part of the parent will be taken to mean that the child is free to behave well or badly. The *moody and sulky* child will respond better to discipline that is quickly over and done with, and where a sense of humour is maintained so that things don't become too serious. These are just a few examples to give you some ideas, but you will have to work out for yourself which type of discipline is best for your child.

2. *The child's age*

Younger children require very clear and straightforward discipline with a high level of control. The words you use should be simple and easily understood and physical restraint may be necessary. *Older children* need a type of discipline that encourages self-control and responsibility. Explanations are required, with some discussion about what the child should have done. Warnings and rewards for good behaviour are helpful. *Teenagers* respond best to discipline that is consistent and continues to maintain the same family standards of behaviour. At the same time the style of discipline should be non-authoritarian, where there is some scope for negotiation and discussion.

3. *Your personality*

Your own personality is bound to affect how you manage your children, but it is important that you don't let the influence of your personality become too great. If you are a *quiet person* by nature, you should be prepared to be a bit more noisy and extrovert sometimes in order to make a greater impact. If you tend to be a rather *emotional person*, you may have more of an effect on your child if you are quiet and controlled in your approach. Should you be a *short-tempered person*, it will be important to try and keep your cool and practise counting up to ten! On the other hand, if you are an *easygoing person* and don't mind too much what your child does, it would probably help if you became a bit stricter. A *loud, extrovert person* who is always laughing and joking may have more effect by being quiet and serious about discipline.

4. *Your own childhood experience of discipline*

One of the most surprising things about being a parent is the lasting effect that your own childhood has on you. It usually comes as quite a surprise to find yourself saying and doing exactly the same as your parents did to you. However, your upbringing may influence you in the opposite way so that you decide that there is no way you are going to put your child through what you experienced. Either way, you are still being influenced by your past.

THE DIFFERENT TYPES OF DISCIPLINE

What type of discipline do you use? It is a good idea to give this some thought. Are you soft and easygoing, or are you a strict disciplinarian? Apart from the perfectly balanced and appropriate discipline that we all aim for, there are three main types of discipline:

1. *Strict and authoritarian*

The child isn't given the benefit of the doubt and very high standards of behaviour are set with little account being taken of the child's individual characteristics. Self-expression by the child is discouraged and the range of acceptable behaviour is restricted. As a result of a strict upbringing, children feel that they can't get away with bad behaviour. They become obedient and submissive, but may complain that they have been unfairly treated. Parents who are too strict run the risk of having inhibited children who may at some later stage become rebellious and resentful towards their parents and others in authority.

2. *Easygoing and indulgent*

With soft and indulgent parents, children usually feel that they can do mostly what they like and have what they want. They come to believe that their own view is just as important as their parent's opinion. If someone says 'no you can't', they become distressed and angry. Children with parents who are too easygoing seem to be self-confident and grown-up, treating adults like equals. Eventually the children become increasingly demanding and are told that they are too big for their boots or spoilt.

3. Inconsistent and unpredictable

This is the most common type of discipline and the most ineffective. However, we all do it because it is impossible to be consistent all the time. Because children are unable to predict what will happen if they do something wrong, they become muddled and confused and in the end will usually do whatever they like.

Treating one child differently from another is a common form of inconsistency, but it can also be inconsistent to treat two children in the same way without taking into account their ages and personalities. What is right for one child may not be right for another with different needs.

If each parent sets different standards of behaviour for the child, even if the difference is a consistent one, the child will be unsure what is expected and will tend to take little notice of either parent. The parent who is the softer of the two will have great difficulty with discipline.

It isn't easy to keep discipline consistent each time you have to deal with naughty behaviour. Maybe you are feeling tired and fed up on one occasion and especially indulgent on another, but if your child can't rely on you to take the same line most of the time, don't expect all that much notice to be taken of what you say.

Most parents use a mixture of all three different types of discipline, but will tend to use one more than the others. Fortunately, so long as both parents are reasonably consistent, discipline has to be extremely strict or indulgent in order to cause any problems. It is inconsistency that is the most frequent cause of ineffective discipline, particularly where the parents set different standards of behaviour.

Agreement between parents is absolutely vital if discipline is going to be effective. If parents find that they differ in their approach, they will either have to agree to compromise and meet each other half way, or one parent will have to change and become more like the other in the type of discipline used and the standards that are set.

Although single parents don't have these problems in quite the same way, exactly the same issues arise if another adult joins the family, when there is a temptation to leave all disciplinary matters to the natural parent. It is a tremendous strain for a single parent to remain consistent all the time as well as working out what the best approach might be each time the child steps out of line.

Even if you have worked out and agreed on your family standards of behaviour at home, it is also important that there is a reasonable level of agreement between you and your child's school. If not, then once again you shouldn't be surprised if there are problems.

GRANDPARENTS AND OTHER RELATIVES

Grandparents have much more influence on children than is generally appreciated. Make sure that they back up your discipline and don't undermine it by being overindulgent or critical. You may have to be very insistent with grandparents because they are likely to think that they know best! Here are some guidelines to consider when coping with grandparents who are interfering:

- Remember that you are the 'boss' now.
- It is 'safer' to be tough with your own parents than with your in-laws!
- You may have to lay down conditions for visiting.
- If there are problems, reduce the frequency and duration of each visit to whatever is tolerable.

- If all else fails, you may have to stop any visits for a while, but try and keep contact by letter or phone.
- A good relationship with grandparents is very helpful for children as they grow up and learn about their own family roots and about growing old; it is worth while making some sacrifices to achieve this.

BEING FAIR

It is obviously important to try to be fair in the way that you discipline your child, but this is easier said than done. What you think is fair and reasonable may not seem that way to your child. Therefore, if anyone says that he thinks that you are not being fair, it is worth while finding out why, just to check whether he has a point. However, children often claim that they are being unfairly treated if they are feeling jealous or angry. Alternatively, they are just being manipulative.

It may sound surprising, but there is something to be said for *not* treating children absolutely equally and fairly all the time because life itself is often unfair and it is best to learn this early on. In fact, if you try and treat children exactly the same, it usually makes them acutely aware of any small difference or inequality and increases feelings of jealousy and rivalry. However, in the long run you should try to strike a reasonable balance so that children don't come to feel that the world is against them.

CONCLUSION

There are many different types and styles of discipline, each of which can be effective if used in the right way, at the right time. Fortunately discipline doesn't have to be perfect all the time, so don't worry too much if you find it all rather difficult. There is quite a lot of scope for making mistakes without causing too many problems for your child. Most children, especially young ones, are remarkably resilient and tough, but maybe that is just as well!

5

. . . . .

Different Methods of Discipline

REWARDS AND PRAISE

We all give a lot of praise and reward to babies and very small children and make excuses when they do something wrong. Certainly it is much more enjoyable to reward than to punish, but in spite of this, as children grow older we become considerably better at noticing bad behaviour and pay less attention to the good things that children do. Once your child has reached school age, try making a note of all the praise you have given in one day and measure it against all the times you have said 'don't' and been cross. You will probably be surprised how little praise and few rewards you give, when compared with tellings off and punishments. This is a shame, because we all respond well to praise, even as adults!

Rewards come in many different forms and parents will have their own which seem to work with their child. Every reward has advantages and disadvantages and the main ones are outlined below:

Attention

Giving attention is the most important and the most effective of all rewards. Attention is much more effective if it is undivided and given without distraction or interruption, so that even a few seconds of undivided attention can be rewarding. However, it is surprisingly unusual for any child to have undivided attention.

Parents are usually doing other things at the same time, such as washing up, cooking, watching TV, or just thinking about what needs to be done next.

Attention can be given in many different ways: a look, a smile, a touch, a cuddle or a few words may be all that is necessary. But if you want to make the attention really special, you will have to do something out of the ordinary and this is where special sessions of undivided attention can be very effective. It is a good idea to be rather formal about any special attention that you give for good behaviour because your child will take more notice of it. For example, rather than patting your child on the head and saying, 'well done', you could shake your child's hand or go into a separate room with strict instructions that you are not to be disturbed for a few minutes while you tell the child how pleased you are. Make a big thing of it and you will be amazed at how it is enjoyed.

Remember that attention doesn't have to be given for very long, provided it is undivided and enjoyable. A few minutes will do.

Unfortunately, children are usually given much more attention for being naughty than for being good, with the inevitable risk that a child's behaviour will become steadily worse in order to get even more attention. It is important to check frequently that you are taking more notice of your child for being good than for being bad (a bit like checking the oil level in the engine of your car!) If the level of attention that you are giving for good behaviour is low, your child might start making a lot of noise or doing something bad in order to be noticed. In which case you will have to look out specially for good things that your child has done so that you can give the extra praise and attention.

Always remember that the attention you give to your child is more effective and in the end more wanted by children than any other kind of reward. All it costs is a little time.

Praise

Parents are brilliant at giving children praise and appreciation for the first few years, but as children grow older less and less praise is given until in adult life it is quite a rare event. When did somebody last tell you what a marvellous parent you are? We all look for clues that tell us we are doing all right. This is one of the reasons why we care so much about what other people think of our children.

As children grow older you will need to become more discriminating in your praise, because it is important that children learn to assess what they have done in a realistic way. You can help your child to do this by giving selective praise and occasional constructive criticism. Imagine a pair of scales with praise for your child in one pan and criticism in the other. Praise should always outweigh criticism, otherwise there is a high risk of your child developing a bad self-image.

Special treats and privileges

Treats are frequently given as a reward for good behaviour, but they are no substitute for attention or praise. It is, however, much easier to hand out a sweet or a toy than to devote time and energy to giving attention. It is best to use treats as a way of backing up and strengthening any praise you give, so that if you give a treat to your child for being good, always give praise at the same time.

It is best to avoid giving food as a reward. Although your child may be pleased at the time, the end result is likely to be a poor appetite at the next meal and, in the long run, an increase in weight. An obese child has a vast range of problems which include teasing, increased frequency of illness and accidents, and a shorter life expectancy. So giving food as a reward may actually turn into a punishment in the end. However, it is very easy for your child to develop the habit of expecting food as a reward and then for this habit to continue into adult life. If you are going to use food to reward good behaviour then try using fruit or even raw vegetables!

Drinks can also be used as a reward, but they have the same problems as food. Perhaps it is best to have one or two things that you use regularly as a reward and keep them just for special treats in order to make them more desirable and rewarding.

Bribery

Bribery sounds rather nasty and unfortunately parents sometimes avoid offering rewards for good behaviour because they think it is bribery. If you are worried about bribery simply change the word 'bribe' into 'reward' and you should feel much better! Don't say: 'I will bribe you with a treat to be good'; say instead 'I will *reward* you with a treat if you are good'.

Love and affection

It is important for children to know that they are loved even though they can do bad things. In other words, it should be possible to love your children while at the same time hating what they do wrong. There is much less risk of damaging a child's self-esteem if a distinction is made between the person and the bad deed.

Obviously, love and affection have a powerful influence on all of us and it is possible to use them as rewards. However, using love as a reward has its risks because children might come to believe that they are only loved when they are good and since most of us spend a lot of time *not* being good, children may easily feel that they are unloved. Therefore it is important to keep the love and affection going all the time, even if you don't always feel like it. An unloved child will feel bad and eventually will probably be bad.

Fortunately, it isn't necessary for parents to have wonderful loving feelings for their children all the time in order to do a good job.

In fact, many parents feel quite hateful towards them at times and a few parents have little affection for their children. In spite of this it is possible to show care and affection without necessarily feeling it.

So long as you are aware of the possible danger of using affection as a reward, there is no harm in giving children a little extra love and care when they do something good. An extra hug, kiss, stroke or touch, together with a few words of praise, can be very effective and the physical contact reinforces what you say.

PUNISHMENTS

In theory it should be possible to avoid all punishments by only rewarding good behaviour and taking no notice of bad behaviour. In practice it isn't possible - you would have to be a saint to do it!

The main problem with punishment is to find something that fits the crime both in severity and in appropriateness. Another difficulty is that it is easy to overdo punishments because you are so keen for your child to be good and because it is easy to get carried away in the heat of the moment, especially if you are feeling very angry. The result of too much punishment is angry and resentful children who feel bad but behave well until adolescence when they tend to become difficult, disobedient and delinquent. However, children who have had too little discipline may also become difficult, disobedient and delinquent in adolescence. So it is important to get discipline as balanced as possible from the very beginning.

Punishments come in many different forms. Here are some of them.

Smacking

It is all too easy to smack a child who has done something naughty. It doesn't require much effort, you don't have to think about it and may appear to be effective in the short run. But, as children grow older, smacking quickly becomes less effective and by the time your child goes to school it will usually make things worse rather than better and tend to build up a feeling of resentment in your child.

A quick tap on the back of the hand may be helpful in the first year or two of a child's life as a means of reinforcing what you say, especially about anything dangerous. For example, if your child continues to try and put a finger in the electric socket, a sharp 'no' accompanied by a smack on the hand when next this happens should help to get the message across. At that age there is no point in telling them about the inherent danger in acting as an earth conductor for high-voltage current! Equally, giving praise for not touching the socket would probably make the child more likely to think that the socket might be really interesting and therefore want to investigate the socket even more closely.

The main problem with physical punishment is that it encourages children to sort out their own problems and frustrations in a physical way themselves, by hitting and punching other people when they are angry with them. A good rule of thumb is that you should stop using this form of punishment as soon as your child is old enough to hit you back – that is, around 2 years of age. Other forms of physical punishment can be used to control very young children. For example, holding a child firmly to prevent damage or to protect from danger. It is important for each family to work out from the very beginning what the rules are going to be for smacking. Both parents must agree on the rules, otherwise their discipline will be undermined and the smack will have no effect or may even be harmful.

Most parents find that they occasionally feel driven to smack a much older child when they have done something really bad. Do try to avoid it if you possibly can, particularly if you are feeling angry, because it can so easily get out of control, leaving both you and your child upset and angry.

Whatever you do, NEVER, NEVER use anything other than your hands to control your child physically, then only on the hands, arms and legs. If you use any object or a fist to smack your child with, you won't be able to gauge how hard you have hit your child. There is a considerable risk of causing physical damage to your child, which is a form of child abuse, but there is also a risk that excessive smacking will cause emotional damage, which is another form of child abuse. We all get uncomfortably angry with our children from time to time, so it is important to think about these things even if they are distasteful.

Remember that smacking is increasingly dangerous and ineffective as your child gets older and that to give more than one firm smack on any occasion is an indulgence on your part. Well, nobody said it was easy being a parent!

Shouting

Shouting, like smacking is easy to do but it soon loses effect and you will find yourself shouting louder and louder until in the end you are screaming, and that isn't much fun for anyone – particularly the neighbours!

If you are going to shout, it is more effective to do it early on, rather than to have a gradual build-up. This slow build-up teaches children to take no notice of you, because they know from experience that there is no need to do what you say until you get really worked up. If you were to make a tape recording of your shouting, you would probably get a terrible shock because it sounds so awful. It is therefore best to reserve your shouting for desperate situations. At least your child will take some notice of you then.

Rather than using up your energy shouting, it is sometimes surprisingly effective to *whisper* very quietly so that your child has to strain to hear. In this way the child is actually more likely to hear what you say. Obviously it is unlikely to work if you whisper all the time; it is the change from the usual shouting that has the effect. If you do whisper, it will be more effective if you speak with a lot of emphasis and in a clipped tone of voice.

Nagging

If your child isn't immediately obedient it is normal to repeat the same instruction again. . . and again. . . and again; in other words, to nag. The trouble with nagging is that it is ineffective, but in spite of this most parents keep on nagging and hoping for a miracle!

What nagging does is to train children to take no notice of what you say because they know that you are going to say it again and again. Nagging also means that you will gradually work yourself up into a state and eventually most parents lose their temper and start shouting. This usually takes children by surprise, because what started the nagging was something that was not very important at all. Another problem about nagging is that it gets children into the habit of waiting until you start shouting and getting cross, so that they soon learn that there is no need to do anything before the shouting starts.

The golden rule about nagging is: DON'T! If you catch yourself doing it, either stop and say no more, or go straight into the shouting/cross phase.

It is a good idea to set yourself the target of only saying things once. If your child doesn't do what you ask immediately, then give a warning. If this still produces no result, then absolutely insist that the child does whatever it is that you have asked. This may mean that you have to get extremely angry and actually make your child do it. The advantage of this approach is that you miss out all the nagging that normally occurs before you become cross and you are putting on a show of being angry before you are pushed to the point of losing your temper and being out of control. At the same time your child is learning that you mean what you say and that it is no good just switching off and taking no notice of what you are saying.

Removing attention

Withdrawing attention is one of the most effective ways of punishing a child and yet this method is rarely used to the full by parents. If your child is doing something very naughty it will of course be difficult if not impossible to ignore it. But most of the time it should be possible, especially if you are sure that your child is safe and can't do much damage if a temper develops.

A strong nerve and a good sense of timing are needed if you are going to ignore a naughty child. If you remove attention from your child for too short a time, it will have no effect, but there is a real danger of ignoring a child for too long. If you do this your child will forget what has been done wrong and begin to feel angry with you instead. Just a few minutes should be long enough and the younger the child is, the shorter the time should be.

Sending a child to another room is a common punishment which removes attention from the child. There are three parts to this punishment:

1. The loss of your attention. This effect wears off in a few minutes.
2. A recovery time for you: 5-10 minutes should be enough.
3. An apology from your child and a discussion of what went wrong.

Many parents make the mistake of thinking that the longer a child stays in the room, the greater the punishment is. This is not the case, because shortly after arriving in the bedroom the naughty child will find something to play with and start to have fun. If you send a child to the bedroom for too long, you end up with a child who blames you for being unreasonable, rather than a child who feels guilty and apologetic.

The recovery time allows you to cool down and feel able to have another go at coping with a naughty child. It is important to remember that any time over 2-3 minutes is for your benefit and is no longer a punishment for your child, while anything over about

10 minutes will breed resentment and make things worse for you in the long run.

As soon as the punishment is finished, the naughty child should apologize for whatever was wrong. Don't expect the apology to be done perfectly, with the right tone of voice and a guilty expression. Just saying, 'I am sorry' should be enough, even if it said with a grumpy voice. Apart from reminding children that they have done something wrong, the apology teaches an important social skill and helps to bring the episode to a close. In this way the bad feelings are left behind and a new start can be made.

Sometimes children are so naughty that they refuse to leave the room when you send them to their bedroom. If your children are small and you are large it is reasonable to physically remove them to the bedroom, but with older children this isn't possible, in which case you could either turn your back on them and be silent or you could leave the room yourself.

Loss of privileges

Going to bed early, being kept in and stopping TV are examples of lost privileges which can be used effectively as punishments, but here again it is important to get the timing and extent of the lost privilege just right. Too little has no effect, too much causes anger. Parents should be careful not to stop their children from doing things that they would actually like them to do. For instance, if you want your child to learn to swim, don't stop swimming as a punishment. If you want your child to be sociable, don't ban friends from the house.

Here are some examples of how you can stop privileges in an effective way:

- Stopping 5 minutes of a favourite TV programme or doing something nice for a shorter time than usual is often more effective than not having it at all.

- Remember to select an appropriate privilege – some children actually like staying in or going to bed early.
- Try to make the loss of privilege occur as soon after the bad behaviour as possible – if it is delayed too long your child will forget what it was all about.
- It is possible to invent a privilege to stop, for example: 'Oh dear! I was going to ask if you would like me to play a game with you, but we won't be able to do this now!'.
- Prolonged loss of privilege will cause resentment, so try to keep it in proportion to the 'crime'. For example, if your daughter comes home 30 minutes after you said that she should, then keep her in for exactly the same time the next day – if she comes back late again the next day too, then you just add that time onto the 30 minutes.

Being angry and telling off

Being cross and angry with a child can be a very severe punishment and quite sufficient in itself. However, it has to be impressive to be effective, which means that you will have to put on a convincing act, but not go over the top. If you become too angry, your child may think, 'Well this is ridiculous – she must be flipping her lid, poor thing!' In other words your child comes to blame you for being too angry and forgets what has been done wrong.

If your child is rather sensitive and highly strung there will be no need to get very angry and there may even be a danger of upsetting the child too much. As a result you will have an obedient but anxious and inhibited child. On the other hand, if your child is thick-skinned you may have to put on an award-winning performance to have any effect. Judging the right level of anger for each child on each occasion is a skill that most parents take years to develop, so don't give up or upset yourself if you can't always get it right.

MAKING DISCIPLINE WORK

There are many different ways of dealing with bad behaviour and it is easy to try one method and give up too quickly if it doesn't work immediately.

It may well be that the method itself is all right but it isn't being applied in a *consistent* way. Discipline is all about *communication*, i.e. giving a clear message to children so that everyone knows that you are serious and that you mean what you say. Although most discipline is based on either giving rewards for good behaviour or punishing bad behaviour, none of this will work unless it is done with loving concern and *care*. Equally, you can't expect to have much effect unless your child *clearly* understands what you are getting at. Clear, consistent communication is helped if it is done with *conviction*. But even if you manage to do all this, you may still not have much success unless you *constantly* stick at it. We therefore have the six Cs of effective discipline:

Constantly Communicate Clearly with
Consistency, Conviction and Care!

It sounds easy and straightforward doesn't it? However, most of us need a lot of practice before we get it right, and, as with most other skills, a lot of hard work is necessary to be able to communicate clearly to your child that you are serious and that you mean what you say.

How to be a good communicator

Communication has many different components that need to be used together if your message is going to get through to your child. Consider the following check-list:

- to start with you must have your child's full attention
- make sure that your child is looking at your face

- the look in your eyes must show that you mean what you say
- your tone of voice must be firm and incisive
- the words you use must be short and to the point
- each word should be very clearly spoken with conviction
- use gestures like pointing or wagging your finger to back up what you are saying
- your manner must be confident and determined.

Don't expect to get it right the first time: most parents require a lot of practice. You will quickly find out whether your act is any good or not by the response. If little notice is taken then more practice is needed, although it could conceivably be that your performance is wonderful and there is something wrong with your child. If you are not sure which way round it is, ask friends to watch your act and see if it impresses them!

CONCLUSION

Praise and encouragement are more effective in the long run than punishments, and children require different styles of discipline specially designed to meet their own unique needs. If the balance of 'do's and 'don't's and of rewards and punishments isn't right and is tipped towards criticism and being negative and hostile, then your child will let you know either by becoming progressively more difficult or by being anxious and withdrawn. Only a few parents find it easy to get discipline right and most of us have to keep working hard at it for years and years, so don't give up – KEEP AT IT!

6
. . . . .

How to Cope with Tantrums and Tempers

Even the most placid child will become angry at times. In fact it is normal for children to go through a stage when they show anger frequently and with little provocation. Children's anger is almost always related to not getting what they want for themselves. So, it is not surprising that tempers are especially noticable at the time when children begin to see themselves as separate individuals. This happens around the age of two to four years.

Loving and caring are opposite to hate and anger, but they can occur together in the same person at the same time, which can be very confusing! All parents naturally use their feelings of loving and caring to counteract any hateful, angry feelings that either they or their children might have. So, the more you are able to help your child to be loving and caring, the less likely it is that your child will be angry and have tempers. But, that said, it is not simply a case of loving and caring for your child enough and everything will be all right. Life is much more complicated than that! Each child has separate and unique needs, which are changing all the time. On some occasions it may be necessary to be very tough and firm with your child, which can also be a way of showing your love for your child. It is surprising how frequently children say, 'I wish my parents would be firmer and stricter with me.'

There are many ways of loving and caring for a child, but one of the less obvious ways is to teach a child self-control. Helping a child to learn how to deal with anger and temper is part of the development of self-control. Children who have learned how to control and manage their emotions and behaviour in a reasonable way, will also have developed self-confidence and good self-esteem.

TEACHING A CHILD HOW TO BE ANGRY

Children have to be taught how to express their anger appropriately. Some parents do not allow their children to show any anger at all and teach them by being very repressive and cross every time the children are angry or aggressive. This approach may work for a few years and a very docile child would result, but eventually the child would probably copy the angry behaviour of their parents and become cross and aggressive themselves.

Other parents get very hurt and upset every time their child becomes angry and take their child's anger as a personal attack. Eventually the child comes to fear the power of his or her own anger and therefore suppresses it. Later on this may lead to the child being inhibited, anxious and passive.

A few parents, however, take little notice of their children's angry outbursts and even laugh at them. If this approach is carried on for a long time the children will have difficulty learning how to control their temper.

Most parents try several different approaches when dealing with their children's anger, tempers and aggression. This can also cause problems because it may be difficult for the children to know what their parents really want.

Should parents 'teach' their child how to be angry? It may seem a strange idea, but if you do nothing, it will probably be other people who do the job for you. Obviously there are 'good' ways of being angry and not so good ways. Here are some ideas about 'good' ways of being angry:

- the anger is a response to something that *most* people would find unacceptable
- the anger is expressed immediately

- the angry reaction is in proportion, to the seriousness of the cause
- the anger is under control, rather than the other way round where the anger controls the person
- the anger does not last much longer than the event that caused the angry feelings
- relationships are not permanently damaged by the anger.

Here are some of the common problems caused by being angry in the wrong way:

- bottled up, suppressed anger will sooner or later cause problems
- anger that builds up and gets out of control can be damaging and frightening
- unexpressed anger may get misdirected, when it comes out at a later stage
- uncontrolled anger spoils relationships

Clearly, it is important to teach children how to manage their own anger in such a way that they don't have these problems, but they are able to express anger effectively.

Perhaps the best way of teaching children how to be angry is to show them by example. Easier said than done, but here are some ideas:

- tell your children when you are feeling angry, so that they know what is going on and what this emotion is all about
- try not to lose control of your own temper. If you are going to get angry, then it is best to 'do it' early on, before things have got out of control. If you are angry in this way you might even be able to enjoy the experience!
- explain to your child what is making you angry, using simple words only
- tell your child what you plan to do to put things right
- be prepared to apologize if you feel you have gone 'over the top'.

It is certainly difficult for anyone to behave like this, but at least this is something to aim for!

Remember that most children's moods do not last as long as adult's moods. They can come and go in a few minutes, so it is worthwhile 'cashing in' on this and making sure that you don't keep the mood going on longer than necessary by being angry and bloody-minded yourself.

It is also worth remembering that the more frequently your child has a temper that goes out of control the more it will become a habit. In fact, after each temper your child will become that much better at throwing a tantrum – until he or she is really expert at it!

AVOID SITUATIONS THAT CAUSE TEMPERS

It is often possible to predict which situations are likely to cause your child to become angry and have a temper. For example, when you tell your child that he or she cannot have a sweet or a toy they ask for. Of course, sometimes it is impossible to avoid these situations, but here are some suggestions that are worth trying:

- a common time for tempers is immediately after an event that has been exciting or tiring, such as returning home after going out, or being picked up from the nursery or school. Plan this time in advance so that you can spend time calming the child and providing extra attention
- when your child has been away from you, even for a few hours, it is a good idea to spend time re-establishing your relationship. One way of doing this is by each telling the other what they have been doing during the separation. If you always do this, your child will eventually get into the habit of telling you things and will enjoy it – even demand it! Talking to each other in this way sets things up for good communication between both of you later on, when it may be really important

- when you are away from home, especially when you want your child to be on his or her best behaviour, tempers are more likely to occur – children seem to know when they have more control over you than usual! They know that you are more likely to give into their demands when in public. It is consequently advisable to keep these times short, pleasant and as much under your control as possible. Try and keep your child occupied and gradually increase the time in public. If you have a set-back and things get out of control, don't panic, just go out for a shorter period next time and gradually build up again.

NEVER BE BLACKMAILED BY TEMPERS

As soon as children realize that they can get what they want by having a temper or even threatening to have one, you have got a problem. If you give in, you are training your child to become an expert in blackmail! If, on the other hand, you stand firm and don't give in, you may also be treated to a temper. But, at least if you stand firm you will be less likely to be threatened in this way in the future and your child will eventually learn that having a temper does not help to get what he or she wants or to win friends.

Of course most parents use blackmail themselves at some time or other, saying, for example, 'I will get cross if you don't stop behaving badly' or 'If you do what I say and you are a good boy, you will get a sweet'. This teaches children all about blackmail and they become rather good at it themselves! You may find it better to be positive and clear and say things like, 'I want you to behave well and this is what I expect you to do . . .' Then be very clear and say exactly what it is that you want them to do.

It is so easy to give in for a quiet life, but this only stores up problems for the future that most of us could well do without. It really is worthwhile being firm and then having the pleasure of seeing this pay off later when your child shows good self-discipline and gets what he or she wants in an acceptable way. It is an important point to remember that self-control and self-discipline have to come from outside first. Children are not born with much in the way of self-control and the only way children can develop this ability is for their parents and other adults to provide it for them until they have learnt how to do it themselves. In this way children gradually learn how to manage their own wishes, desires and feelings.

GIVE DISTRACTIONS AND WARNINGS

If you see your child working up to a temper, it helps if you can get in quickly and distract the child, but this will only work if you intervene early enough. Watch out that your distractions are not just a form of blackmail in disguise or your child will soon learn to work the system – just threaten a temper and along comes an interesting distraction!

If you see a child heading straight towards a temper, it is easier to gently steer the child off course rather than to go off in a completely different direction, which usually requires a major distraction that may be seen as a reward for threatening a temper.

Here are some simple examples of distractions that you can try:

- getting the child to do something helpful is a good idea because it is difficult to have a temper and be helpful at the same time! For example, a child says, 'I want my meal now!' and you respond 'Yes, just help me lay the table' or 'Let's go and have a look at the clock and you can help me see if it is teatime yet . . . Oh look, it is 3 o'clock, it is time for . . . (whatever you have planned to do)'
- giving a running commentary on what is happening around you can often prevent a temper from developing. 'We are just going to cross the road now and we are looking both ways to make sure nothing is coming. Look at the boy on the bike. Is it clear now? Off we go then. Listen to the noise of the lorry. Here we

are on the other side. Which way are we going now?' Because
you are going on and on and on, the child will usually be
distracted from moodiness and tempers
- asking questions will sometimes work. The child stops to think
  of the answer and, because it is difficult to concentrate on two
  things at once, there is a good chance that the moodiness will
  be forgotten, at least long enough for the child to be distracted
- many parents find it helpful to use toys as a distraction. Make
  sure that they are easily available, so that you can immediately
  provide the distraction before things get out of hand and early
  enough for the toy not to be seen as a reward for threatening
  a temper.

Giving a warning to your child can be helpful in preventing anger
and tempers building up and getting out of hand. Do be careful
to give a warning that can be carried out easily otherwise your child
will quickly learn that you don't really mean what you say. Here
are some examples of warnings that are difficult to carry through
or make things worse in other ways:

- 'If you have a temper I will smack you'
  There are three problems here:
  1 smacking is likely to teach a child how to be physically
  aggressive
  2 even if you feel that smacking is acceptable, it is difficult to
  carry it out in public because other people are likely to make
  comments
  3 smacking usually makes tempers worse rather than better
- 'I will tell your father if you have a temper and he will punish
  you when he gets home'
  The problem with this type of warning is that the result is too
  delayed and probably unpredictable, because the father may not
  feel like being angry and punishing the child
- 'I won't let you out to play for the whole day if you have another
  temper'

This type of warning can be difficult to keep because it means having a rather fed-up child at home all day. Children quickly learn that if they moan and groan and are difficult enough when being kept in, then most parents will relent and let them out, just to have a bit of peace and quiet. Also, strange as it may seem, some children actually enjoy being indoors

- 'If you have a temper you won't be able to have a sweet'
  Although this may work once or twice, most children will soon learn that they can get a sweet very easily, just by threatening a temper.

But don't be put off by these disadvantages. It is helpful to be aware of the problems so that you are less likely to make the mistakes that all of us make at times. There are many advantages of giving a warning and here are some of them:

- a warning makes it clear that you want from the child
- it tells the child what the consequences are of not doing what is expected and what has been asked
- when the consequences happen it makes more sense to the child
- you will feel better because you are doing what you said you would do, rather than being pushed by your child to do something on the spur of the moment and then regretting it afterwards.

Perhaps the most important thing about giving a warning is to be sure it makes sense and if it is linked to a threat, that you are prepared to stick to it. So why not try some of the following suggestions:

- 'If you carry on like that there will not be enough time left to play a game with me'
- 'If you don't stop by the time I count three I will leave the room'
- 'If you continue like that you will be so tired you will have to go to bed'

- 'I am leaving the room until you have stopped all that noise'
- 'If you want to do something nice (that you have already arranged) then you had better not have a temper'
- 'If you think you are good at tempers, wait till you see me get into one!'

Each warning uses a slightly different approach. Every child will vary in his or her response to warnings, depending on temperament and the situation. It is obviously important to carry out any threat you make, otherwise you won't be taken seriously. Sometimes children get used to the warnings and take little notice. So it is a good idea to vary them from time to time.

Sometimes it can be more effective to use a joke warning. This works partly by being different and therefore more noticeable, but joke warnings also work because it is not easy to laugh and be angry at the same time. An added advantage is that if you like your own joke it will help you to keep your cool. Here are some examples of joke warnings just to give you an idea of what you might say if you can't think of anything yourself and to show you that it is not necessary to be a brilliant comic:

- 'Watch out! Stamping your foot like that is hurting the floor. Did you hear it cry out just then?'
- 'You are not shouting loud enough. Please stamp your foot harder and shout louder . . . No, louder than that . . . No, even harder! . . . Is that the best you can do?'
- 'If you shout any louder the penguins in the South Pole will hear you'
- 'Your stamping is making the house shake . . . I hope the roof does not fall in'
- 'You sound like a parrot when you go on like that.'

Obviously joke warnings can make things worse, but at least it is under your control, and the joke, however pathetic, often changes the focus of the anger. A joke warninig can also be a way of showing the child that you are not very impressed with the temper and you are not going to take it too seriously.

EXPECT AN APOLOGY

If all your efforts at trying to prevent the temper have been unsuccessful, *don't worry!* You are in very good company. Every other parent has had the same problem! There is still a lot that can be done to help your child after the temper has finished.

When the temper is over it is helpful to expect your child to apologize. This signals the end of the anger and helps the child to carry on normally rather than going on sulking. The temper is put in the past and the child is able to make a new start. An apology also helps to re-establish good relationships and to put things right again after the outburst.

Making up after an argument or outburst of temper is very important for everyone concerned. It teaches children how to finish an argument without finishing the relationship, which is obviously an important skill to learn before adulthood.

REMOVE ALL ATTENTION AND ISOLATE

In spite of all the good intentions and plans, things don't always work out as you would like them to. Sometimes, whatever you do seems to have no effect or may even make things worse. Maybe you are not feeling too good yourself or your child is particularly determined to be bad tempered. What then?

Have you ever noticed that children rarely have an outburst of temper when they are on their own? Temper tantrums are performed for an audience. So if you leave the child in a temper, even if he or she is screaming and kicking on the floor and walk out of the room, the temper will be unlikely to carry on much longer.

Removing attention from your child can be very difficult if the child is causing damage or injury. If you feel it is too risky just to leave the child where she is, then you will have to remove your child to where it is safe. The bedroom is often the safest place for a child to be on its own, but some parents feel it is wrong to use the bedroom because it should be a comfortable place. However, the most important reason for using the bedroom is because it is safe and the child can be left there without attention for a few minutes.

See Chapter 7 on Special Techniques to back up your efforts at discipline.

WHEN IT ALL FALLS APART!

If all else fails and the temper gets right out of control, you may have to hold your child. Never attempt to hold a child in a temper unless you are sure that you are strong enough to be in total control. Holding a wriggling bundle of anger is not much fun for you, but could be great fun for the child if it becomes clear that you are losing control and he or she is winning the 'contest'.

Most parents would find it fairly difficult to hold down a child on their own when the child is aged five years or older. It all depends on size and strength, but think carefully before you tackle an older child (who, in any case, should have grown out of tempers by that age).

Holding a child in a temper is a high-risk business! There is a risk that either you or your child will get hurt and almost certainly the temper will get worse before it gets better. There is no way of telling when is the best time to hold a child, except to say that it is when the parent feels it is right. This technique is not right for every child or every parent, but it can be extremely helpful in some cases.

Here are some step-by-step guidelines for holding a child in a temper:

- your child must be out of control or nearly so
- you should feel that holding is the right thing to do
- give your child a warning so that he or she has a chance to regain self-control
- warn other people what you are planning to do
- sit the child on your lap, facing away from you so that your face cannot be seen and so that the child does not get extra attention
- put your arms around the child's middle and, with your left hand, hold the child's right wrist. Then, with your right hand, hold the child's left wrist
- now cross your child's arms over so that your arms are uncrossed. To do this you will have to pull firmly but only hard enough to keep them in position on either side of the child's hips
- your child's legs should be between your legs, which should be crossed at the ankles so that you can grip the child's legs firmly enough to prevent them thrashing around
- when your child wriggles and struggles, you should tighten your grip just enough to control the child and prevent an escape. When the child calms down you can relax your hold. But don't leave go and be prepared to tighten your grip if there is another struggle or wriggle
- once you start holding your child it is important to see it through to the end – when your child has calmed down either through exhaustion or because it is clear that you are determined to be in control and the child realizes that there is no point in continuing in a temper
- you will have to continue the hold for as long as it takes, which may be minutes or hours
- one possible way of bringing the holding to an early end is to tell the child to be still while you count up to five and if he is still you will let go. However, it is generally best to talk as little as possible to your child during the holding
- finally, make sure that your chin is not near the back of the child's head in case you are knocked out with a backwards head-butt!

Well, it sounds rather like all-in wrestling and very complicated. Holding a child in this way is better than being pushed into a temper yourself or going over the top and smacking or beating your child. This holding method works by showing your child that you are in control and that you can safely cope with his or her anger. In the end your child will not only feel more secure and safe, but will also have learned something about self-control. This type of holding is not for everybody, so only use it if you feel comfortable and confident about it.

81

7

. . . . .

Special Techniques

Here are some techniques that you can use to back up your discipline and make it more effective. The methods are well known, but have to be used correctly to produce any results, so I will explain each one in some detail.

PREVENTION IS BETTER THAN CURE

There are a lot of things you can do to avoid your child being difficult and disobedient. Obviously, being firm and clear in your discipline will make naughty behaviour less likely to occur, but here are some other points to consider.

Setting a good example

Children quickly learn to follow the example set by older children and adults whom they respect. In fact, setting at good example is one of the best ways of achieving good behaviour and avoiding the need to use discipline. It is always important to be careful that you're not punishing your child for something that you do or that someone else in the family does and gets away with. This would be unfair and undermine your discipline.

Supervision

A great deal of bad behaviour occurs when children are unsupervised and away from your watchful eye. This is one way of finding out how successful you have been in setting standards of behaviour. If you hear that your child is well behaved when away from you at school or with friends, then you know that you are doing a pretty good job!

Young children need almost total supervision during the daytime, but as they grow older it can be difficult to know how quickly to ease off and allow more freedom. In fact, the only way of finding this out is by trial and error. It is important to build up trust gradually and give your child increasingly more responsibility.

With the distractions of the radio and TV and the demands of everyday life, it is easy to cut down on supervision and to give children too much freedom too early. So if you or other people find your child's behaviour difficult or disruptive, an increase in adult supervision is the first thing you should consider. It may well be that your child's naughtiness has more to do with lack of adequate supervision than with a need for more discipline. Have a think about it!

Organizing the environment

A lot of bad behaviour can be prevented by arranging your home so that it is safe for children. Here are some ideas for 'structuring the environment' to make it less likely that your child will do something naughty:

- use a playpen for children up to 2 years old
- put your favourite ornaments out of harm's way
- keep the TV, video and hi-fi out of reach, unless you don't mind the knobs being fiddled with
- use a box or cupboard to keep toys safe

and for older children:

- put an alarm on the larder door if food goes missing!
- don't leave money lying around
- avoid your child having too many toys to get lost or broken
- insist on headphones if the music is too loud

These are just a few ideas to show you how you might go about organizing your home to make life easier for you and so that you don't have to be cross with your child quite so frequently.

Habit training

Getting dressed and undressed, washing, sitting at the table for meals, going to the toilet and going to bed occur every day and frequently cause arguments. These disputes can be avoided by training your child from an early age to accept the events as a regular routine so that they become an automatic part of everyday life that requires no discussion or thought – in other words they become a habit.

If your child is causing problems with two or more of these daily tasks, it is probably best to look at it as a habit-training problem. In which case you will have to be much more insistent and firm about keeping to a regular routine and doing things in the same way each day in order to get a good habit established. If this doesn't work you need to be even more insistent and do everything by the clock. It is well worth keeping at it until you have got it right, because in this way you will avoid all the difficult behaviour which occurs several times each day.

'At risk' times

Children are much more likely to be naughty and disruptive if they are bored, hungry, thirsty or tired. All of these conditions can be avoided with some advance planning and thought. Again, it is helpful to have a regular daily routine that avoids these problems, by planning meals, snacks, playtimes and rests.

THE ART OF TIMING

If you return home and hear that your child has done something bad, your natural reaction is to be upset and angry. Try to change your feeling of being upset into sadness rather than anger, because in this situation sadness is much more effective and it will allow you to have a quiet talk with your child about what went wrong and how the naughty behaviour can be avoided in future. Delayed praise from the returning parent can also be effective in backing up what has been said about good behaviour that occurred earlier in the day.

There are occasions when the time isn't right to discipline your child. For example, on a special occasion, that would be spoilt by having to be cross or where your child might feel humiliated to be disciplined in front of friends. In these cases it is best to leave it until a more appropriate time and then discuss the event with your child and express sadness rather than anger. Another time when it may be best not to discipline children is when they are ill, but here again timing is all important because it is vital to judge the correct time for restarting discipline. If you leave it too late your child could become a little monster in no time at all. If you get it right, the return to normal discipline is a very reassuring sign to your child that he or she is getting better.

To punish a child is always a sad event which is distressing for all concerned. It is therefore a good idea to spend some time and effort making things right afterwards. When you feel that the time is right, discuss briefly with your children what has happened, so that they can learn from the episode (3 or 4 minutes is quite long enough). Children should learn to apologize for their bad behaviour as this helps to make them more aware that they are responsible for it and that they can't put the blame on someone else. However, it is good to set an example to your child by apologizing if you have gone a bit over the top or done something wrong.

Perhaps the most important aspect of timing discipline is knowing when to stop. Most parents give up rather easily when the method of discipline that they are using doesn't seem to be working. Don't give up, but rather think, am I doing it right? If you think that you are, then keep at it! The methods of discipline that I have described in this book can be expected to bring about an obvious improvement in 4–6 weeks if you apply them correctly, consistently, and confidently. Perfection takes a little longer!

STAR CHARTS AND RECORDS

Keeping a diary or record of naughty behaviour can be very helpful if you're not quite sure why your child is being disobedient and difficult. Often the reason will become clear when you, or perhaps someone else reads your observations. It may be helpful to use the ABC method of recording as follows:

A = antecedents, i.e. whatever happened before the behaviour
B = behaviour, i.e. the naughty behaviour
C = consequence, i.e. what happened as a result of the behaviour.

The ABC method is a good way of helping you to think about what exactly caused an episode of bad behaviour and it is not unusual for parents to find that they are actually keeping the problem behaviour going without realizing it, for example by giving in to children who behave badly. After a week or two you may see a pattern emerging which will show you what is going wrong and may give you ideas as to how to change things to improve the behaviour.

Star charts give a less detailed record of behaviour and don't have to involve stars at all. The chart divides the day up into separate periods. If the child is good during any period, a star is put on the chart to show that the behaviour was good. If the child has been bad then the chart space is left blank. However, instead of stars you can use ticks, smiley faces, little drawings, stickers or anything else that appeals to your child.

The idea behind a chart is very simple – rewarding good behaviour – and it may seem artificial. However, there is more to a chart than you might think:

- The stars may become very powerful rewards in themselves
- The focus is changed from the bad behaviour to concentrating on good behaviour.
- A chart diverts attention and anger away from people and onto the chart.
- A chart helps parents to be more consistent.
- The chart acts as a record of what progress is being made.

Children between the ages of 5 and 12 usually respond well to charts, but it is important to make it into something special and interesting and to involve your child in the organization of the chart as much as possible. Try to make it good fun and something that your child can be proud of.

The chart should be divided into periods that are short enough for your child to remain well behaved – with a bit of effort on a good day – so that it is not too difficult to gain a star. At the end of the day, provided your child has tried to be good, there should be more stars than spaces. As soon as you feel that your child has got the message and is regularly being well behaved, the stars should be made a bit more difficult to achieve. This can be done by gradually increasing the duration of each period or by expecting more from the child before a star is gained. Whichever way round it is, your child must at all times know exactly what has to be done to achieve a star. One of the most difficult things with a chart is to keep it going and keep your child motivated. You will need all your ingenuity to keep your child interested in the chart. Here are some ideas:

- Put the chart in a prominent position such as the kitchen or dining room wall.
- Involve other family members or friends in praising the child for any success.
- Give the stars a value, e g. 1p per star, or 5 stars gaining the child a privilege such as staying up a bit later one night, having a story read, or playing a game. Don't make the stars worth too much, otherwise it can get completely out of hand!

Most charts work well for a day or two but then things slip back into the bad old ways unless you work hard to keep the chart going. Aim to have the chart for a fairly short time, such as 1-4 weeks. If things are no better by the end of this period, try reading the Help! section on page 134.

POCKET MONEY

As soon as your child has some understanding of the value of money, it is helpful to give a small amount of pocket money. Pocket money is useful for the following reasons:

- teaching the value of money
- learning to delay gratification
- teaching children that actions have consequences
- giving a child the feeling of being more independent
- to increase self-control
- to encourage saving
- to teach your child about giving and generosity.

Clearly there are other ways of achieving the same goals, but pocket money is convenient and can be very effective if managed correctly. It is best to keep the money limited to a small amount and then gradually increase it as your child grows older. At the same time children should be expected to do more with the money and to be more responsible for their own needs and for buying gifts for others.

One way of organizing the amount of pocket money would be to start with 10p a week at 5 years old and increase by 20p a year up to 10 years of age. Then increase by 30p a year up to 15 years of age and finally at 15 years old start a clothing allowance which can cover other things as well. There is no point in giving large amounts of pocket money, because the more you give the more your child will want. There will always be someone else that your child knows who gets more money and who will be quoted to you whenever your child wants more money, but don't be fooled by this ploy. However, it is important that you help your child to feel content with the pocket money and to use it wisely, rather than spending all the time feeling envious of others and grumbling for more money.

When your child is older, a clothing allowance can be very helpful in encouraging independence and responsibility. It is a good idea to set the amount low to begin with and then review it after 3-6 months. Meanwhile your teenager should keep a detailed record of every item bought and then present it to you with the receipts at the end of the review period. If you are satisfied that all is well, then you can consider whether an increase is justified or not. It may be best for you to buy the clothes for school so that at least you know that the basics are all right.

Once you have got the pocket money well established, it can then be used for discipline in the following ways:

- If your child does something good then there could be a small bonus with the pocket money at the end of the week.
- Doing something bad can be dealt with by a deduction from pocket money, but young children may not remember what they did wrong if the time gap is too large between the event and the deduction.
- If you have made a deduction of pocket money for whatever reason, it is a good idea to hand your child the full amount each

week and then get him to hand back the required amount. This will help your child to be fully aware of what the deduction was all about.

- Be careful not to undermine the pocket money by giving extra things that should normally be bought by your child. It can be very revealing to add up the cost of all the extra treats you give during one week – you will probably get quite a surprise!
- Many children are impulsive and even reckless with their pocket money when it first starts and it all goes in a few days. If this is the case, it may help for your child to be given the money more frequently, perhaps twice a week but preferably not every day because this won't encourage your child to learn how to control money and delay gratification.
- Pocket money can be used for paying fines for bad behaviour, but it is especially useful for paying towards the cost of breakages and damage caused deliberately by your child or through carelessness. This helps children to become more aware of the consequences of their actions and helps you to deal with the situation without becoming too upset and angry.
- It may also be helpful to have a savings account to accompany the pocket money. Not only does this encourage saving, it is also useful as back-up for buying special items or paying off fines quickly.
- Any extra money given by friends and relatives is best collected and put into your child's savings account, otherwise the money will probably be frittered away.
- One parent should take responsibility for organizing the pocket money to make sure that it is given regularly and that deductions are made when necessary.
- Try to avoid stopping the money completely. Even prisoners have a small amount of pocket money!

'TIME OUT'

The procedure for removing attention and isolating children when they have been naughty is sometimes called 'Time Out', which is a technical term for excluding a child from having any attention or reward. It is a form of punishment that is particularly popular in America, but even so I don't think there is any evidence that American children are any better behaved than other children. So Time Out doesn't perform miracles, but it can be useful. In fact parents often use a form of Time Out without realizing it when they send a child out of the room or to bed early for doing something naughty.

Time Out should be carried out on a carefully planned basis, where you start by identifying a specific, unacceptable behaviour, *the target behaviour*, and then planning how you will remove attention in a predetermined way whenever the bad behaviour is observed. There are two main varieties of Time Out that parents can use.

1. Attention Time Out in a separate room. Here children are removed from the situation in which they are behaving badly and sent or taken to a room where they will get no attention. They are then left there for a specific number of minutes. Alternatively, you can remain in the room but ignore your child or you can leave the room yourself.
2. Activity Time Out. Here children are not allowed to join in a particular activity, or told to stop whatever they were doing. They aren't asked to leave the room, but are expected to remain to see what is being missed.

The period of isolation should be timed by the clock and is usually for a few minutes only. One minute per year of age would be a reasonable guide. However, the main impact of Time Out is in the first few seconds when children realize that the parent is displeased to the point of wanting to ignore them. The Time Out procedure is then repeated as often as it is necessary to have the desired effect. Here are some ways of making sure that Time Out is effective when you use it:

- Decide in advance which room is going to be the place where you send or take your child to for Time Out. The room must be completely safe for your child to be left unsupervised for a few minutes. Usually the bedroom is a suitable place.
- Make sure that you time the period of Time Out accurately and stick to what you have decided.
- Sending your child out of the room may be just as effective as isolating him or her in another room.
- Even turning your back on your child can be an effective form of Time Out.
- Your child must be quite clear which bad behaviour it is that you are 'timing out' and it is best to work on one specific bad behaviour at a time, or your child might spend most of the day in Time Out!
- When the Time Out is completed, an apology from your child is a good way of signalling that the episode is over and done with.
- It is best to put aside any discussion about the event until quite a while after the Time Out.
- You can make the most of Time Out by not becoming cross or emotional. In fact, Time Out works best if you are firm and tough, and when you are able to keep your temper.

There are many problems in using this rather rigid approach to discipline. Even the name 'Time Out' tends to give the impression of a technical procedure and it is sometimes used to describe an extreme type of more prolonged and total isolation which is not appropriate for a family home. Here are some of the problems to watch out for when using Time Out:

- Some children actually prefer to spend some time away from the situation which they have caused. In this case the Time Out is a reward and will have the reverse effect of that intended.

- Other children may resist being 'timed out' and continue to behave badly and to attract even more attention. In this case another type of discipline would be better, especially one that uses rewards.
- Time Out only teaches children what they should NOT do, rather than what they SHOULD do. So don't forget to tell your child exactly what sort of behaviour you would like and, if you get it, don't forget to praise it!
- If the Time Out is too long your child is likely to become angry and resentful and forget what the Time Out is for.
- The Time Out must occur immediately after the bad behaviour if it is to be effective. Delayed or repeated Time Out for one episode of bad behaviour sows seeds of resentment.
- Time Out is difficult to organize when you are away from home. If you do carry it out, don't forget to warn everyone first, otherwise they may wonder what you are up to!
- If you use Time Out too frequently it will lose its effect, so use it sparingly and concentrate on one particular naughty behaviour at a time.

SPECIAL DIETS

The idea that you are what you eat is both attractive and fashionable. Many parents have had the experience of excluding food additives, red meat, milk, wheat germ and other food stuffs from their children's diet and noticing an improvement in behaviour. It is therefore surprising that almost all the well-conducted scientific research has shown that food additives and normal foods make no difference to behaviour. Could it be that all this research, carried out in many different countries round the world, has somehow got it wrong?

A likely explanation for the positive effect of dietary restrictions is that parents are usually very strict about it and perhaps for the first time say 'no' to their child in a firm and definite way. Certainly it is not unusual for disciplinary control in one area to improve a child's general behaviour.

If you still want to try to see whether a change of diet will help, it is important to do it properly. This means conducting your own experiment, which needs to be done in 2-week stages. This is because changes of behaviour are said to take about two weeks to respond to alterations in diet. Here are some guidelines:

- Keep a daily record of your child's behaviour.
- Remove the suspect foods completely for two weeks.
- If an exclusion diet appears to help, then go on to the next stage.
- Replace one food at a time at 2-week intervals and if the behaviour becomes worse again the food can be excluded from the diet for a longer period.
- When you have decided on the flnal diet, make sure that it isn't unbalanced. Get professional advice if you are in any doubt. Some special diets can cause nutritional deficiencies.
- It is a good idea to use an independent observer who doesn't know what diet your child is on, but observes the changes in behaviour, just to be quite sure that you aren't imagining any improvement.
- You may be able gradually to get your child back to a reasonably normal diet, so it is worthwhile reintroducing the excluded foods from time to time, just to check if they are tolerated without a deterioration of behaviour.

KEEPING A SENSE OF HUMOUR

The whole business of discipline can get a bit heavy and serious if you are not careful. Try to keep a sense of humour about discipline – it's much more fun! A humorous punishment can sometimes be more effective than a serious one because your child is more likely to remember and learn from it. A sense of humour is a very personal thing, so you will have to think up your own kind of funny discipline. The joke is as much for you to enjoy as for your child, because it will help you to stay relatively calm and not lose your temper. Discipline carried out in a temper is very rarely effective for more than a few minutes, so have a bit of fun instead!

CONCLUSION

Discipline is a form of training and is essential if you want your child to become socially acceptable and to develop self-control. The emphasis should be on learning to do the right thing, rather than just stopping bad behaviour. Start from the very beginning with firm, strong discipline so that your child learns what the limits are: this is an important way of showing your loving care. As your child grows up and by behaving well earns more responsibility, you can then allow more freedom. Although there are many useful methods of discipline, the most important thing is to be confident in what you do and to follow things through, but above all try not to lose that sense of humour!

8

· · · · ·

Questions and Answers

These questions and answers are organized into two parts. The 'Yes but . . .' section is for parents who maybe do not fully agree with what I have said. They have got their own ideas, which are, or at least seem to be, different from mine. The 'What if . . .' section is for parents who generally agree with what I have said but can see all the problems and pitfalls.

YES BUT . . .

'My son has been difficult from the moment he was born and I don't seem to be able to change his bad behaviour. What should I do?'

It is increasingly recognized that some babies are born with a difficult temperament. The so-called *'difficult child'* is easy to identify, because he or she has the following characteristics right from the start:

- *unpredictable;* usually difficult to feed, put to bed or to toilet and then sometimes easy
- *very strong emotions;* with tempers and crying, rather than being happy
- *easily disturbed by change;* slow to settle and difficult to comfort.

It sounds as though you have a child with a difficult temperament, in which case you will immediately recognize these characteristics. If this is the case, you have a tough time ahead of you! But don't despair, there are things that you can do to help your child and many children will have grown out of it before they start at school. Many children will fit the description given above, but it is possible to distinguish between children who are born with a difficult temperament and other children who have been allowed to learn how to get attention and get their own way by being difficult, because the problems are present from birth in the former case and not in the latter.

These children with a difficult temperament require 'extra super' parenting if they are to be helped, so it is not going to be easy. They need more of the following than you would normally provide:

- routine and regularity
- clear limit setting
- high level of supervision
- firm, consistent, loving discipline
- frequent comfort and reward.

If you are able to provide this extra care, most children will learn to modify their temperament reasonably well by the time they start at school. But some children will continue to be difficult with behaviour problems and then it is just a case of carrying on with the guidelines above with determination and increased intensity.

It is most important to balance this rather controlling form of care with a great deal of positive care and love. Otherwise you will find that you are forever getting at your child and saying things like: 'stop it', 'be quiet', 'come here' or 'don't'. Many parents find it difficult to be loving towards a child who is frequently irritable and disobedient. Your son will probably have many bad experiences because he is naughty, so you will have to work at it. Here are some ways of balancing the negative experiences that a child with a difficult temperament will go through.

97

- Try to avoid situations which you know your son will be unable to cope with without being very difficult and temperamental. These occasions only give children practice in how to be difficult and annoying! However, if it is something like getting dressed in the morning or going to the toilet, you obviously can't avoid it. In this case, a regular routine is helpful so that your child becomes used to doing things automatically, and knows that arguments and tempers are pointless.

- Look out for any good thing that your son does, especially if he manages to control his temper in a satisfactory way; also give as much praise as you can. Don't worry about going over the top with your praise, it won't do any harm!

- Deliberately set up situations with which you know your son should be able to cope without being difficult and behaving badly so that you can give praise and encouragement, rather than telling him off yet again.

- Arrange special times for your son to be alone with you or with another trusted adult, purely to enjoy your time together. This is *High Quality Time* which is many times more worthwhile than being together in the ordinary way, when you have something else to do at the time, for example the washing up, the cleaning or making a meal.

'What can I do with my daughter who always seems to be doing naughty things?'

I assume that you have decided that your daughter doesn't have a difficult temperament like the boy in the previous question. Even so, the same guidelines will help, together with all the things I have outlined in the book. If your daughter is aged 7 years or older, it may be that she has developed a bad self-image, which in turn will lead to bad behaviour. The main signs of a poor self-image are as follows:

- deliberately doing bad things in an obvious way in order to get caught
- seeming to get pleasure from being told off
- appearing to be uncomfortable when praised
- deliberately spoiling anything that is good
- talking about being bad and not feeling as good as other children

If your daughter has these characteristics it is important to first work out how this has happened. It can only occur if your child has had a lot of bad experiences. Do make sure that this is not still happening. Children with a bad self-image can be helped by using the same approach as that for the difficult boy described above, but remember to keep the praise going even if it is rejected.

The *High Quality Time* is especially helpful to a child with a poor self-image, so here are some guidelines for getting the best out of this special time.

- Do something that you both enjoy, such as a game, playing outside, going for a walk, or just talking together.
- Make sure that there are no distractions, such as the TV, or disturbances, such as other people coming into the room.
- Keep this special time short and intensive so that you both finish while you feel that you would like to do it again. Five minutes of high quality time every day or even every few days may be quite sufficient and better than many hours of ordinary time.

This special time will remind your child that she is indeed special and that what she does is important to you. In other words you are showing that you care for your child and love her, in spite of everything.

'What should I do if other children come to my house and behave badly?'

It is helpful to have very clear *house rules*. These are rules that have to be obeyed by anybody who is in your home. Don't change your rules just because you have visitors, but warn them about the rules if you think there are going to be problems. Most children will accept this arrangement if it is made clear to them before things get too out of hand. If they still don't behave, you can always send them home early!

'My daughter claims that I am much more strict than other parents'

Most children use the example of their friends to try and get a better deal for themselves at home. There is always someone who is given more toys, more pocket money or more freedom than your poor hard-done-by child! It is worthwhile considering whether your child has a point. However, if you feel that you have got it right, there is no need for you to change. Just explain that your family has well-thought-out rules of behaviour, and that is how it is going to continue. Most children accept this quite well and even feel more secure because of it.

'My child is very placid and never seems to get angry'

Children vary a lot in temperament and it is quite possible for a child with an easygoing temperament to experience very little anger. On the other hand, anxious and sensitive children may not show much anger because it frightens them, but they feel anger strongly and quickly sense it in other people. If a child is a slow developer he or she will be delayed in reaching the stage when

anger and tempers become obvious. In the slow developer there
will be little sign of anger and tempers until the child has reached
the developmental stage of a 1½–2 year old.

---

*'My child has terrible tempers even though he is now
6 years old'*

Tempers and bad behaviour are more common in boys than girls,
but you would expect children to have a reasonable control of their
temper by the time they start school at the age of 5 years. At 6
years of age a temper should not last much longer than a few
minutes or occur more frequently than once every few days. It is
difficult to be more specific because tempers are so dependent on
the circumstances in which they occur. However, if your child is
still having frequent or very bad tempers after starting primary
school, there must be something wrong somewhere. It may not be
serious, but it needs to be dealt with. The longer a child continues
to have tempers, the more difficult it is to change.

  Here are some reasons why bad tempers might not improve as
your child gets older:

- your child has a difficult temperament: if this is the case the
  child will have been difficult from birth – if not before!
- you have not been able to be firm enough in helping your child
  to gain control of tempers and anger
- you have been inconsistent in your response to anger and
  tempers, so the child has not been able to learn how to manage
  anger
- the child has witnessed a lot of anger and tempers in the family
  and has come to believe that expressing anger is the best way
  of getting what you want and being noticed
- the child has got into the habit of having a temper as soon as
  a feeling of frustration develops. The angry response habit is
  both automatic and unnecessary, but very difficult to stop.

'I think that all children should express their anger freely'

It is a common notion that it is good to express anger, but it is not as easy as that. If children are allowed to express their anger freely and without any check, before they have learnt how to cope with it, their anger and aggression will grow and get more and more out of control. Anger needs to be 'managed' and expressed in a reasonably controlled way. There are even some occasions when it is in a child's best interest to keep feelings of anger under check – for example, when with a teacher or other person in authority.

'Suppressing angry feelings only stores up problems for later on'

Yes, suppression of anger is not a good idea. It is nevertheless important that children learn to manage their anger so that it can be expressed at the right time and without getting out of control. But, as mentioned above, there are a few times when it is just not worth showing anger, when it would only make things worse. Children have to learn when these times are and how to first recognize anger and then to use the unexpressed anger in a constructive way.

'If anger is not brought out into the open, it is stored up and comes out some other way'

Not necessarily. Anger and other moods don't behave like physical forces and they don't obey the laws of physics. Very strong anger that is only expressed in a mild way, may not leave a store of anger if it is dealt with immediately, before it is allowed to get out of control. Sometimes it is possible for anger to just fade away over a period of time. On the other hand, a small amount of anger that is allowed to fester, may gradually build up and eventually come to the surface over some very insignificant event and be quite out of proportion.

'My mother says I grew out of my temper without her having to do anything, so why should I worry about my daughter's tempers?'

Your mother may be right, but make your own decision and do what you think is right for *your* child. The danger of doing nothing is that your child may never learn how to control her temper and by the time you find this out it may be too late to do much about it.

'I have done everything you say . . . but it doesn't work!'

Well done! It is difficult to stick to doing the right thing all the time and to be consistent, but if that is what you are doing, keep at it and it will work in the end. The guidelines that I have given are tried and tested and can be expected to be successful if applied in a consistent and determined way. If you have done all this for several months without any improvement then something is wrong somewhere. Maybe all your hard work is being undermined by another person or perhaps your child really is very difficult. Think about it carefully, discuss it with a friend, read this book again and if you are still stuck, this is the time to get some professional help.

'I hardly agree with anything you have said'

Well, everybody is entitled to his own views! I have already said that there are a wide range of ideas about childcare and many different ways of bringing children up. There is no 'best way' because each individual has different needs. What works with one family may not work with another. I have tried to outline what the main issues are and what the mechanisms are, so that you can work out the details for yourself as they apply to your own situation. If your children are still young it is possible to make lots of mistakes without too much of an immediate effect on them. It is later on, as the children approach adolescence that any earlier mistakes in child-rearing tend to become more obvious.

The ideas and guidelines in this book are based on a lot of people's experience and the results of research. All I can say is that the approach described here is more likely to work with most children than any other.

'Do teenagers need to be dealt with differently?'

Almost everything that I have put into this book applies to children of all ages, including teenagers. As children grow older their problems tend to get bigger with them and as they enter adolescence moodiness and defiance tend to become more marked. About half the behaviour problems of the teenage years are a continuation of earlier childhood problems; the other half occur for the first time. Fortunately the majority of teenagers manage to reach adulthood without too many problems. It may seem surprising, but most teenagers actually have much the same views on politics, religion and moral standards as their parents.

The levels of female and male sex hormones begin to rise roughly two years before there are any signs of puberty. This means that children as young as 8 or 9 years old may experience the behavioural and emotional effects of these hormones, which tend to make boys more aggressive and assertive, girls more emotional and moody. These physical changes, together with the pressures of increasing self-awareness, are major factors that cause the rate of behaviour and emotional problems to double during adolescence. The most dramatic changes of all are seen in a fourfold increase in anxiety and depressive states.

Although teenagers can be demanding and exasperating in the way they carry on, it doesn't help to get too steamed up about them or to let them wear you down. It doesn't go on for ever, so it is mainly a question of how to survive during the stormy times. Here are some suggestions that may help:

- *Teenagers need to be treated seriously, but not taken seriously.* In other words, keep a sense of humour and don't let them get you down. At the same time, your teenager should think that you are treating him or her really seriously.
- *Say your bit, then leave it.* Try and avoid arguments. It is better to make your point simply and clearly and then leave your teenager to think it over.
- *React with sadness rather than anger.* A sad reaction to any misbehaviour is far more effective than blowing your top. Try it and see for yourself, even if you have to act the part.
- *Teenagers are not really independent adults until they have left home.* They still need a great deal of your time, care and supervision - more than they would care to admit.
- *Better to be a block of concrete than a trampoline!* It is best to try and avoid going up and down with your teenager's moods. You can help by continuing to set the same standards, to say the same things and not to be distracted from the beliefs that you feel are important. Staying solid as a block of concrete will reduce your teenager's ups and downs. If you climb on their 'emotional trampoline' and try and go against them, you will both fall off. If you go up and down with your teenager, you will both hit the roof. Do you get the picture?
- *Provide a safe harbour to protect from the storms of adolescence.* What teenagers need most is to be surrounded by consistent care, calm and stable relationships. Adolescence can be rather like being tossed around in a tiny boat out in a stormy sea. It is therefore reassuring for young people to have parents who act like a lighthouse, showing the leading lights to the harbour that is always there and always safe.

WHAT IF . . .

'My son is rude and swears'

Children quickly learn that being rude produces interesting reactions in other people. It is not unusual for adults to laugh at rudeness in very young children because it is so incongruous, but this only makes it more likely for the child to be rude again. Children will imitate swearing if they hear it at home or outside the home. So if you swear yourself, don't be surprised if your child does too. If you want him to stop swearing, you will first have to stop everyone in the family from swearing!

Like so many kinds of bad behaviour, rudeness is best nipped in the bud, before it becomes a habit. Here are some ideas about what you can do to achieve this:

- Make sure that your child isn't successful in using rudeness or swearing to get your attention or to wind you up.
- You could try ignoring your child completely until he has said the same thing in a polite way and apologized for being rude.
- A strong and immediate overreaction to swearing can be helpful in making it quite clear that this is unacceptable. Being strong doesn't mean smacking, which should be avoided; it means being very clear indeed that rudeness is just not on. If your child still takes no notice, you obviously need a little more practice at being convincing!
- Older children (7 years +) may find it helpful to pay 5-10p for the luxury of using each swearword, with the proceeds going to a children's charity.
- It is much more difficult to control swearing outside the home, and it is therefore best to concentrate on getting it right at home so that your child knows right from wrong.

'My child steals money and other things'

Most children take things without asking at some time or another, but stealing needs to be dealt with firmly and clearly, even if your child is very young. The trouble with stealing is that it is one of the very few behaviours that is immediately rewarding. This makes it likely to happen again in spite of being found out. The most common reason for stealing is because the opportunity is there and it is possible to get away with it. So if you leave money lying around, or you collect money in a jar on the mantelpiece, don't be too surprised if it disappears. Stealing is increasingly more serious the older the child, especially after the age of 8 years old. Before you start to deal with stealing it is important to think about the possible underlying causes, as follows:

- you haven't made it clear that taking without asking is wrong
- your child has got away with stealing in the past
- you leave things lying around and make it easy for your child to steal without anyone knowing
- sometimes children take things for themselves if they are feeling miserable, jealous and/or angry
- occasionally a child will steal on the instructions of someone else, for example to pay off a bully at school
- children who find it difficult to make friends may 'buy' friendship by giving away things that they have stolen
- some children steal in a gang and may be led astray by others.

There are three important steps to take in order to deal with stealing effectively:

1. Prevention
This involves keeping money out of the child's sight and if necessary even locked up. It is only reasonable to leave money lying around if you are certain that your child doesn't steal.

2. Detection

It is important to have a system of checking so that you know if and when your child has stolen. This may mean keeping an account of the money in your bag or pocket and checking through your child's things so that you are aware of anything new that appears that can't be explained. Don't feel guilty about checking your child's personal possessions, because it is unreasonable to trust someone who is stealing.

3. Restitution

Restitution involves making things right again. So anything that has been taken has to be returned with an apology. If 10p was stolen then 10p is returned. If a toy was stolen, the toy must be returned. If something was taken but then lost or used up, the same should be returned in value or in kind. Your child should never be allowed to keep anything that has been stolen. If your child is paying back from pocket money it is best to hand over all the money and then get your child to hand back the necessary amount so that it is clear that some of the money is being taken away. It is also a good idea to leave your child with some pocket money rather than to stop it completely (see page 88).

The punishment for stealing is for your child to be found out and to know that you are upset. The apology and return of the stolen property is also part of the punishment. No further punishment should be necessary. If you do anything too tough it may make further stealing more likely out of anger and resentment.

Any child who steals should have regular pocket money so that it is possible to pay back anything that has been stolen. An account book should be kept because it teaches children the value of money and where it all goes. It will also help you to be able to keep a check on what is happening with your child's money. No further pocket money should be given until you have checked that the book is up-to-date and correct.

It is also helpful for a child who steals to have a savings account where a proportion of the pocket money is saved, together with any other gifts of money. The money is saved for something special that your child particularly wants and then, if there is any further stealing, the money for paying back comes directly from the savings account. In this way the stealing is dealt with quickly.

If your child continues to steal in spite of sticking to this programme, you will have to increase the level of supervision even further. It is a good idea not to trust your child while stealing is a problem and not for six months after the last episode of stealing. It will take this long to build up trust again.

Stealing outside the home can be dealt with in much the same way, but a higher level of supervision is required. It may even be necessary to accompany your child whenever he or she goes out of the house. This may seem a bit excessive, but if you are half-hearted in the way you deal with stealing, you will only be half successful!

'My child is hyperactive'

Hyperactivity is not a bad or naughty behaviour because it isn't done deliberately, as can be seen from the following list of causes.

- Hyperactivity and restlessness is a normal stage of development between the ages of 2 and 6 years. In some children, especially boys, this phase can last even longer.
- Distressed children who have had to cope with a lot of family stress tend to be more restless and unsettled.
- Children who have been allowed too much freedom to do as they please are often restless and demanding.
- A few children, especially those with some sort of brain disorder such as epilepsy or birth injury, are hyperactive due to a medical condition called either 'the hyperkinetic syndrome' or 'attention deficit disorder'.

- Children who are overstimulated and overexcited will be hyperactive.
- Lack of sleep can cause children to be overactive.
- Although there is no firm evidence, it is possible that particular foods and additives make children restless.

Hyperactive children benefit not only from dealing with the cause if possible, but also from routine and regularity in everyday life, with firm boundaries set for their behaviour. Concentration exercises can help – you could ask your child to concentrate on a task for a few seconds, timed by the clock, and then gradually increase the time over several weeks, always ending each concentration session on a note of success.

'My son is very destructive'

All children go through a destructive phase at some time or another, but there are several possible causes for destructive behaviour:

- On the whole boys are more often destructive than girls.
- Some children (especially boys) are more clumsy by nature and therefore more likely to break things accidentally. It is no good getting cross and upset if this is the case because it won't help and it may even make things worse. Clumsy children need extra supervision and practice at being careful, together with praise when they get it right.
- Younger children are naturally more clumsy and destructive, so it is unfair to give them rather delicate or sophisticated toys to play with and then get upset when the toys are damaged.
- Sometimes children will be deliberately destructive if they are angry or jealous, but if this is the case the choice of target will be obvious. The best method of dealing with this is to get the child to replace whatever has been damaged and give an apology.

If the cost is high then money can be earned by doing extra jobs around the house.

- Children with a poor self-image sometimes go out of their way to be destructive and deliberately damage things. It is important to recognize this cause of destructive behaviour, because nothing will make things better unless the child's self-image is improved (see page 98).
- Distressed children who live in a disorganized, unpredictable and insecure environment are often destructive in a particular way. They tend to tear up their clothes, bed clothes and wallpaper. They mix things together and make a mess and they may even be destructive to themselves. It is a worrying sign if these behaviours continue and it indicates that a radical rethink is necessary about how things are organized at home.

It is important to distinguish between accidental damage which requires no punishment and deliberate destructiveness, where some form of restitution is necessary. In other words, try and make the punishment fit the crime.

'My daughter tells lies'

Like the understanding of right and wrong, the concept of lying only develops gradually and is not well established until 8-10 years of age. Younger children need to be taught that it is wrong to tell lies, but older children require some form of discipline for lying. The most effective form of punishment is for your child to be found out and for you to be upset and disappointed.

It is important to develop the skill of detecting when your child is lying so that she doesn't get away with it, because this is the most common reason for lying. Some children are more difficult to 'read' than others, but every child will have some telltale sign which will give her away; it is just a question of knowing what it is.

If your child has got stuck in the habit of telling lies, think about the following questions:

- Why hasn't your child learnt that it is wrong to lie? Has she been slow learning other things as well?
- Can your child tell lies and get away with it?
- Does your child steal as well, because stealing and lying often go hand in hand?
- What has your child got to hide? Is she afraid of your reaction to the truth?
- Do you trust your child too much?
- Has your child got some other reason to tell lies, such as wanting people to believe that she is a better person than she thinks she is?

If your child regularly tells lies, it is best not to believe what she says until you have checked for yourself that the story is correct. Children who lie should know that they are not believed and that trust can only be built up by telling the truth.

'My son lights fires'

Fire-setting is obviously dangerous and should never be allowed to happen at all. This means training your child right from the beginning about the dangers of fire. If, in spite of your training, your child lights a fire without your permission, your reaction should be so memorable that it never happens again. It isn't unusual for children between the ages of 4 and 6 years old to experiment with fire, without knowing how dangerous it is. So at these ages it is particularly important to keep matches and fires well away and to give a high level of supervision and training.

Children who repeatedly set fires have one or more of the following problems:

- the child is poorly supervised
- there are problems in the relationships at home which have caused the child to be distressed and to want to draw attention to himself
- insufficient training about the danger of fire has been given
- the fire setting is part of a wider behaviour problem and indicates serious disturbance
- lighting fires may have become something of a habit, a way of having excitement from watching the fire and everyone's reaction to it, especially if the fire brigade is called.

Children who set fires over the age of 6 years old are a particular cause for concern. A very high level of care and supervision is needed.

'My daughter behaves badly in a sexual way'

Children will copy the sexual behaviour that they see around them, and will generally adopt the standards that their parents set. However, the TV and videos can also be very influential. Adult sexual behaviour is clearly inappropriate in a child, so it is important to keep this side of your life to yourself. At the same time it is important to teach your child what sort of sexual behaviour is acceptable at different stages of development.

If your child behaves in an inappropriately sexual way, you should consider the following possibilities:

- Has adult sexual behaviour or talk been witnessed at home?
- Has your child seen adult sex on the TV or video?
- Has your child picked up ideas from other children?
- Could she have seen pornographic magazines?
- Is it possible that there has been some form of sexual abuse?

Each cause has a fairly obvious solution, but if you believe that your child has been sexually abused it will be necessary to seek expert help.

'My son plays truant from school'

Playing truant can be distinguished from school phobia because in the latter case the parents know where the child is, but with truancy neither the parents nor the teachers know where the child is. As a general rule, children who play truant on their own are more disturbed than when it is done in a group. However, all truancy should be a cause for concern, particularly if it is from primary school.

There are several possible reasons why children hop off school:

- The school is boring or difficult for the child and seems to have nothing much to offer.
- Your son is being led astray by other children (why is your child so easily led?)
- The school is disorganized and doesn't check up on truancy.
- Truancy may occur where the parents are preoccupied with other problems, such as marital difficulties or both parents working.
- If your son has other antisocial behaviour as well as truancy, it probably means that he has quite serious problems and is out of your control. Perhaps you need some specialist outside help.
- Maybe your son isn't getting enough supervision. Communication between home and school needs to be tightened up, perhaps with the help of a daily diary that goes between home and school.
- Sometimes children play truant because they have found something much more interesting to do, such as a paid job or meeting a friend.

As soon as you find out that your child is playing truant, it is important to work out which of the various factors are causing the problem and to have a meeting with the school. It helps to have a system worked out with the school where they agree to contact you if your child doesn't turn up. It may even be necessary to keep a check at every lesson and for the child to stay with a teacher at break times.

'My daughter keeps bad company and is easily led'

Peer group pressure is a powerful force to reckon with, but even in adolescence most children will follow their parents' views when it comes to the crunch. Some parents feel that they have no right to interfere with their children's friendships, but equally parents have a right and indeed a duty to protect children from being led astray. It is therefore entirely reasonable for you to be quite intrusive and if necessary intervene in a potentially damaging relationship. Obviously this is a delicate area and you will need to be careful but not over-sensitive about it.

'My son sniffs glue'

Glue-sniffing and abuse of other substances is extremely dangerous and worrying. It indicates that there is something wrong if it happens more than once and it is better to see the problem as having more to do with failure and distress than with bad behaviour. The following failures are commonly associated with substance abuse:

- unsatisfactory relationships at home and outside
- academic failure at school
- a breakdown in communication at home and/or between home and school
- a failure to supervise adequately

- low self-esteem and a feeling of failure.

The underlying causes need to be dealt with, together with the provision of a high level of supervision and loving care. The problem is complicated, however, and outside help is frequently required.

'My children argue and answer back all the time'

It is always difficult to get the balance right between allowing children freedom to speak their mind and not letting them be opinionated and bloody-minded. If you feel that the balance is not quite right with your children and your friends agree with you, then you will have to do some determined work and take a tough stand in order to get any change. Children easily get stuck in the habit of arguing and answering back so that it happens automatically without the child realizing it. If you want to break the habit, it is no good being subtle or half-hearted – you will have to go for it in a big way!

'My child is aggressive and fights a lot'

Fighting and aggression are not unusual for young children and a lot will depend on what standards of behaviour you set. If marked aggressive behaviour continues much after starting at school, then there are likely to be serious consequences. It is helpful to have a low threshold for unacceptable aggression and then to keep to it. The least show of aggression over the limit is then immediately dealt with. The risk of continued aggressive behaviour is so great that a very determined and firm line needs to be taken. Much the same approach is needed that you would use to stop a child running into the road.

- Set a good example yourself.

- Keep telling your child what is expected.
- Show your child the right way to be assertive.
- Supervise closely until you are sure your child can manage alone.
- Any aggression must be stopped immediately.
- Most children need repeated practice until they get it right.
- Teach your child how to be caring and generous.

Some children get into a habit of reacting aggressively and this can be difficult to stop. Nevertheless the approach outlined above should be effective if you keep working at all the suggestions and teach your child to be thoughtful about other people's feelings.

'My son is difficult to get out of bed and makes a fuss about getting dressed'

Getting up and dressed is one of the important habits of everyday life that should be well established before a child starts at school. Some children need more time and extra training to develop a good habit - perhaps your child is one of these. In order to institute a good habit it will be necessary to insist that your son repeats the appropriate behaviour over and over again until he has got it right. Normally this would be done each morning, but there is no reason why it should not be repeated several times on the same day, if you think it will help.

When children are smaller it is possible to show them how to get up and dressed by physically taking over and doing it for them. If this is done in the right way, most children will eventually prefer to do it themselves. Older children may respond to time limits, for example, being at the breakfast table by a certain time or being dressed before an alarm clock rings.

If a child who has previously had no problems in getting up in the morning suddenly changes the habits of a lifetime, it is likely that all is not well. Assuming that this is not due to physical illness, it is probable that emotional distress of one sort or another is the

117

cause. If the problem goes away at weekends and during holidays it is safe to suspect that the problem is school-related and that your help is needed to sort it out.

'My son says I am unfair because other parents give lots of sweets and treats'

It sounds as though your son is good at persuasion and has learnt how to use words rather than tempers to get his own way. You should be pleased with yourself! However, if you follow what your child claims other parents do, you could soon get into a muddle – partly because it may not be true and partly because the other parents may have got it wrong. You should do what you feel is right for your child and not do something just because other parents do it. It is a good idea to teach your child right from the start that what other parents allow their children to do is irrelevant as far as you are concerned. What matters is what happens to your family and *you* decide what the rules are rather than your son.

'My wife and I don't agree with each other about how to cope with our daughter's tempers'

When parents don't agree on how to deal with tempers, each will cancel the effect of the other and there is little point in trying to do anything about the tempers until you can agree. Usually one parent takes a tougher line and the other a softer one. The stricter parent tries to be a bit tougher to compensate for the other's softness, but then the easygoing parent becomes even more indulgent to balance the effect of the other being too strict. In this way the parents' attitudes become polarized and what began as a slight difference between the parents grows into a big one and agreement is difficult if not impossible to reach.

It is vital that you reach some agreement. Otherwise the whole family will suffer. It would probably be best to try and reach a compromise, but if this is not possible then one of you will need to make the main decisions and the other will just have to go along with it and be prepared to back up the decision maker. Either one or both of you will have to change.

'I can't even control my own anger'

We all find it difficult, but somehow or other you will have to learn to control it, otherwise there is little chance of your child controlling his or her temper. As you might have guessed, almost all the things that I have said about tempers and anger apply to adults as well. So you can work on it together!

'I can't avoid some situations that I know cause my daughter to have a temper'

It would never be possible to avoid all situations that cause tempers and it would not be a good idea anyway. Children have to learn to cope with frustration. At least you will know in advance which situations to watch out for and, if you plan in advance, things should not get too out of hand. It might even be a good idea deliberately to set up a situation where you know your daughter is at risk of a temper and help her to cope with it by talking about it before, during and after the event. This may sound a bit cold and technical, but at least you are helping your daughter to learn about the management of anger and if she is successful you can both celebrate!

'The distractions and warnings have stopped working'

Try some others! As children develop and change, so should your response to them. But you are quite right – as children grow up they become more difficult to distract away from whatever they intend to do. So you have to rely increasingly on all the hard work you have done with your child in earlier years. Certainly you will have to be careful that your distractions don't become more and more exciting or your child will soon learn how to work the system! At the same time, if you find that your warnings are becoming increasingly severe, it is time to review why your child is not learning how to manage anger.

'My son continues to sulk for hours after a temper'

Sulking is to a large extent part of a child's temperament and, like other aspects of personality, it is possible to 'shape' and change it to some degree. Teaching children to apologize helps to stop bad moods carrying on. If your son continues sulking in spite of everything, then it is best to take no notice at all and act as if things are quite normal. If all else fails, try tickling! It is important to set a good example for your son and make sure that he sees you dealing with your anger quickly and not letting it drag on. Don't forget other members of the family, because if they are good at sulking they will undermine all your hard work.

'I worry that my 4-year-old son will harm himself because his tempers are so violent'

Some tempers can be quite frightening, but remember that tempers usually stop if there is no audience. A few children do have very bad tempers, but screaming and shouting will not do them any harm – it only exhausts them. No bad thing perhaps! Occasionally children deliberately hurt themselves during a temper to show everybody how serious it is. Biting and headbanging is not unusual.

In most cases this type of self-injury fades away quickly, once children realize that they are not getting attention or any other form of reward for this behaviour. Therefore, it is best to ignore your son should he start to hurt himself during a temper. Easier said than done, of course, but with a bit of advance planning and thought it should be possible. If your child were much older than 4 years of age, then self-injury would be more serious. This is partly because it indicates that anger is not under control and partly because it is much more likely that the child is in a seriously distressed state.

'My son breath-holds in a temper'

This is not unusual for young children, either at the beginning, or at the end of a temper. The child may go red, white or blue; he may go stiff or floppy, but after a few seconds he will start breathing again. Children normally grow out of this by the age of 4 or 5 years, and the less fuss you make of it the better. Breath-holding can be very frightening the first time you see it, but ordinary breath-holding associated with a temper is self-limiting – it will stop more quickly if you do nothing about it.

Sometimes it is even possible for breath-holding to lead to unconsciousness and there may be twitching of the arms and legs. Don't panic. If it is caused by the temper, the less you do the better. Rarely, this can be caused by an epileptic fit. Fits are not usually associated with tempers and the unconsciousness continues for longer than with the breath-holding. Get medical advice if you are in any doubt.

'My daughter is sometimes sick during a temper'

This is not unusual in young children and there is a danger that they will realize that it is a good way of getting attention and do it again. For this reason it is best to clear it up, giving as little attention to your daughter as possible, apart from a comment like 'How disgusting' or 'What a mess', depending on how deliberate you feel the vomiting was.

Parents worry that their child may inhale the vomit, but the risk of this is very small. If the child is still screaming with temper after being sick, there should be no reason to worry. But, if there is silence and your child is known to be sick easily, then it is worthwhile checking that all is well. Try to do this with as little attention to the child as possible.

'My child is too strong to hold in a temper'

Most parents can cope with holding a child up to the age of about 5 years old. At this age the worst of tempers should be over. Remember, never attempt to hold a child who is in a temper unless you are confident that you are strong enough to see it right to the end - when the child has calmed down and has apologized.

APPENDIX 1

. . . . .

What the Research Shows

Difficult and disruptive behaviour has been studied extensively and there is now good agreement on the main facts, which I will outline here. Research has also identified the main factors that are associated with tempers and anger in children. I hope that you will be able to use this information when you are wondering why your child seems to be naughty and whether other children are just as badly behaved.

Several different terms – such as *conduct disorder, behaviour disorder, antisocial* or *deviant behaviour* – are used for behaviour that has got out of hand and is causing distress. They all refer to behaviours that are outside the range that parents normally regard as acceptable. As for anger and aggression, much of our everyday understanding of these emotions stems from the work of the psychoanalysts. Freud, Jung, Klein and others highlighted the importance of anger as a normal, and sometimes unconscious, motivating force. A great deal has been written about the psychoanalytic view of the child, who is portrayed as being at the mercy of unconscious aggressive and pleasure-seeking impulses. This view may seem compelling, and it has shaped the way many people understand anger in children, but unfortunately there is little or no research evidence that supports it. In fact, psycho-analytic theory is impossible to prove or disprove because it is based on assumptions about the unconscious mind which are, by their very nature, untestable.

SURVEYS

F. L. Goodenough (1931) was the first to carry out a detailed survey of tempers. She observed a large group of American children aged from 1-7 and also persuaded their mothers to keep a daily diary of the children's behaviour. Tempers were found to occur more often at bedtime, at the end of the morning and the end of the afternoon. It was assumed that these were the times when the children were hungry or tired.

After the age of 2 the episodes of temper gradually became shorter and less violent, but whining and sulking increased. Overall, the main causes of tempers were attempts to get the children to conform to accepted standards of social behaviour and relationships.

Subsequent surveys by J. W.MacFarlane et al. (1954) in California and Naomi Richman et al. (1982) confirmed F. L. Goodenough's findings that tempers are frequent in children aged from 2-5, with a peak around 2-3 years old.

Naomi Richman and her colleagues conducted a survey of 3-year-old children in Walthamstow, London, and found that 7 per cent had moderate or severe behaviour problems. Her findings also reported that tempers and difficult behaviour are more common in boys than girls and that difficult behaviour tends to persist. In fact, about 70 per cent of the children who had significant behaviour problems at 3 years of age still had them a year later.

A very important survey of children aged 10-11 living on the Isle of Wight was carried out by Professor Michael Rutter and others. They used parent and teacher observations together with detailed interviews of the children. About 25 per cent of the children were noted to be disobedient at home, but at school less than 10 per cent were disobedient; 4 per cent of the children were found to have a serious behaviour problem that was severe enough to be a handicap. As in most of the other surveys, more boys than girls were reported to have bad behaviour (Rutter et al., 1970).

A survey of children aged 7 years old in New Zealand found that

20 per cent showed some form of antisocial behaviour such as destructiveness or disobedience, with or without hyperactivity, and 9 per cent had behaviour problems that persisted (McGee et al., 1984).

Although these studies might seem to show that bad behaviour increases with age, this is more likely to be due to a parent's changing perception of what is unacceptable at different ages – and the fact that larger children can make more of an impact!

An epidemiological survey done in Buckinghamshire (Professor Michael Shepherd et al., 1971) found that tempers and aggression were still quite common in older children, especially in boys. Professor Shepherd et al. noted that 10 per cent of 5-year-old boys had temper tantrums at least once a week, but the same frequency of tempers was only reported in 2 per cent of 15-year-olds. However, irritability and other forms of angry behaviour tended to continue. It would seem that, although tempers tend to *decrease* with age, there is no evidence that children's experience of anger diminishes in any way – it just changes the way it shows itself.

The Isle of Wight and Buckinghamshire surveys found that reports of children's moodiness and feelings of misery tended to increase in frequency as the children grew older. Of 10–11-year-olds, 12 per cent felt miserable and this had doubled by the age of 14–15. So, while anger becomes less obvious, depression becomes more apparent in older children.

TEMPERAMENT

Alexander Thomas and Stella Chess (1977) carried out a classic study of a group of children in New York. They looked at nine temperamental characteristics and noted that the following were associated with an increased frequency of difficult behaviour, including tempers and irritability:

- irregular, unpredictable eating and sleeping habits

- strong, mostly negative moods
- slowness in adapting to new situations.

Similar findings were reported by Professor Philip Graham et al. (1973) in London. They identified a temperamental adversity index, using the characteristics isolated by Thomas and Chess. The index was able to predict those children who were likely to have problems a year later. A high score gave a threefold increase in the risk of difficult behaviour at home and an eightfold risk of problems at school. Children who demonstrated the characteristics from birth onwards were often said to have 'the difficult child syndrome'.

Judy Dunn and others (1981) found that children with adverse temperamental characteristics were more likely to react badly to the birth of a sibling. Dunn's other (1977) study noted that the same group of children were more likely to have accidents.

It is probable that it is not just a case of children behaving in a particular way because they have a certain type of temperament. It is more likely to be an interaction between the children and their environment, most notably their mother or principal carer.

THE INFLUENCE OF THE FAMILY

Patterson (1982) has described antisocial behaviours in children and aggressive behaviours in parents that lead on to a predictable sequence of events called 'the coercive system', as follows:

1. Badly behaved children make it difficult for their parents to use the more subtle forms of management of deviant behaviour and to encourage good behaviour.
2. The naughty child frequently produces an aggressive response from the parent, which then serves as a model or example for the child to follow. Alternatively the parent may give in 'for a quiet life', in which case the child will learn that it pays to be bad.

126

3. The level of disturbance and aggression in the family rises and anarchy follows, leading to a further break-down of caring and positive, helping behaviours in family interactions.
4. As a result, the parents tend to become fed up and irritable. They lose their confidence and self-esteem and their children also become frustrated and fed up.
5. Family members disengage from each other, the parents become disunited and the control of antisocial behaviour breaks down, resulting in still further problems – and so the cycle continues.

The association of various family factors with antisocial behaviour has been reviewed by Sula Wolff. She found that the following factors were statistically linked to conduct disorder (Wolff, 1985):

- absence of the father
- loss of a parent through divorce rather than through death
- a depressed mother
- an irritable parent
- marital discord
- socioeconomic disadvantage
- large family size.

Each of these factors could be the cause or the result of the bad behaviour and it is difficult to tell which comes first. For example, having a difficult child would be enough to make any parent irritable and a hostile parent could make a child feel angry and frustrated. What usually happens is that a vicious cycle develops between the child and the parent, each making the other more hostile and upset. The immediate effect of these influences is more obvious in boys, but there is some evidence that girls may show more adverse effects in the long term (Rutter, 1982).

Naomi Richman's 1982 study found that the following family and social factors were associated with behaviour problems in children:

- marital difficulties

- maternal depression
- large family size
- living in rented accommodation.

The British Births Survey followed up all the children born in the UK on or between the 5th and 11th April, 1970. Using data collected when the children were 5 years of age, Jean Golding and D. Rush (1986) reported that approximately 10 per cent of children were reported to be often disobedient and 'quick to fly off the handle'. Forty per cent of 4–5 year olds had tempers, of which 13 per cent had tempers at least once a week. Overall, boys had more temper tantrums than girls. Frequent tempers were more likely to occur if the children:

- had young or elderly mothers
- came from single-parent households
- came from step-parent households
- lived in poor social conditions
- were growing up with poverty and unemployment
- came from a household of more than three children
- had mothers who smoked heavily
- were living in an inner-city area
- were living in the Midlands or North of England
- had a low birth weight

Children with temper tantrums were also more likely to have the following problems:

- bed-wetting
- soiling
- feeding problems as a baby
- sleeping problems as a baby
- hyperactivity
- general difficult behaviour
- feelings of misery

- speech and language difficulties
- headaches and stomach aches
- frequent sore throats and wheezing

The above lists of statistically significant associations must be interpreted with care. For example, the link between tempers and mothers who smoke heavily may be a direct one - the effect of inhaled cigarette smoke on the child - or it may be a case of a difficult child causing his mother to smoke more. Alternatively the link might be an indirect one - poor living conditions causing stress reactions (tempers in the child and heavy smoking in the mother). Usually the links are due to may different factors, each interacting with all the others in very complicated ways.

Other Factors

Although family factors play a part in the development of bad behaviour, other causes have also been identified (McGee et al., 1984; Barron and Earls, 1984, 1985):

- babies who are smaller than expected size for their gestational age
- brain damage, whatever the cause
- poor verbal ability
- specific rending delay
- hearing difficulty
- two or more changes of school in the first two years
- stressful life events
- poor housing

Bad behaviour therefore has highly complex relationships with a wide range of family and social influences. To some extent the child plays only a small part in the generation of problem behaviours, yet it is the child who normally takes most of the blame!

BEHAVIOUR PROBLEMS AT SCHOOL

Bad behaviour also occurs in a school context, where it has been shown that the most frequent reason for suspension is aggressive behaviour (Nicol et al., 1985). Boys are more likely to be excluded from school than girls and, once excluded, very few children return to normal schooling (Galloway et al., 1982).

Children with specific reading problems have consistently been found to fail at school and to have a higher frequency of behaviour problems when compared with children who have no difficulty with reading. Most studies suggest that there is an extremely complicated relationship between the bad behaviour and the reading problem, with both having some causative factors in common (Rutter and Madge, 1976).

The school itself may have characteristics that encourage or at least allow the development of antisocial behaviour (Reynolds and Sullivan, 1981). Several studies show that even if school intake factors are allowed for, there remain consistent differences between schools in the rate of antisocial behaviour seen in the children. The most likely explanation for these differences is that they have been caused by the school. They include the following factors:

- low staff morale
- high teacher turnover
- unclear standards of behaviour
- inconsistent methods of discipline
- poor organization
- lack of awareness of children as individuals.

ANGRY BEHAVIOUR

Apart from the early work on tempers, there is not much research that looks specifically at the angry behaviour of children as they grow older. The focus tends to be more on overt aggression than anger. Of course there is a close link between the two emotions, but anger is about the frustration of not having your own way while aggression is more concerned with damage to people or property and is not always associated with anger.

An interesting study from the US by E. M. Cummings et al. (1984) investigated how children reacted to anger between their parents. Toddlers commonly reacted with distress or anger – even if the parents' anger was simulated. On the other hand, school-age children reacted more frequently by comforting or intervening in the argument. Some children consistently reacted more than others and this continued to be the case over a period of five years.

Children's responses to affection between their parents were also studied, and angry, distressed behaviour was again noted, although the main reaction was one of pleasure or affection-seeking themselves. Interestingly, it was noted that angry incidents were reported two or three times more commonly than episodes of affection. This study supports the notion that parental behaviour is important in determining how children feel and behave.

H. C. Dawe (1934) analysed 200 quarrels between 40 preschool children in a day-nursery and found the following:

- boys were more aggressive than girls
- most of the arguments were about possessions
- children tended to argue less as they grew older
- children became more aggressive as they grew older
- the average number of quarrels was three to four per hour
- most arguments were very short-lived, lasting about 20 seconds
- most arguments were sorted out by the children and caused little or no resentment

The finding that angry quarrels are so frequent and brief at this young age is interesting, and although the study was carried out many years ago there is no reason to think that children have changed much.

WHAT HAPPENS TO CHILDREN WITH ANTISOCIAL BEHAVIOUR?

The sociologist Lee Robins (1978) carried out important long-term studies of antisocial children in the US and found that some 90 per cent of antisocial adults engaged in similar behaviour as children. This worrying finding is balanced by the finding that about half of the antisocial children did not grow up into sociopathic adults and this type of behaviour in preschool children does not usually lead to similar problems later on.

It does seem, however, that from school age onwards anti-social behaviour has a strong tendency to continue as a very stable characteristic that may be difficult to change (Olweus, 1979). Philip Graham and Michael Rutter (1973) studied secondary school children and found that over a period of three years, 50 per cent of the children with bad behaviour continued to cause problems.

The following factors have been found to be associated with a poor outcome for antisocial behaviour in children (Kelso and Stewart, 1986):

- frequent bad behaviour
- aggressive, argumentative and disruptive behaviour
- fire-setting
- mixing with other antisocial children
- truancy and lying
- growing up in extreme poverty
- misuse of drugs
- running off
- early onset of problems
- a wide range of behaviour problems
- other members of the family showing antisocial behaviour
- a history of alcohol problems in the family

CONCLUSIONS

The research findings suggest that as children grow older there is a strong tendency for bad behaviour to persist, even into adult life. Family influences interact with the child's characteristics in such a way that the child is predisposed to develop antisocial activities. This in turn leads to rejection and isolation of the child by others, resulting in a deep sense of anger and frustration and further bad behaviour. Eventually, as the child grows older, a poor self-image is formed as well as a strong feeling of failure that fuels that vicious cycle. This pessimistic outcome need not occur if the factors leading to problem behaviours are understood and something is done about them early on, while the child is still young.

Research findings are a bit like a jigsaw puzzle: a certain bit of information may be the missing piece you have been looking for that makes sense of the whole – or none of it may seem to fit together at all. I have outlined some of the main findings that hopefully may give you a picture of your child's behaviour. Yet it is doubtful whether all the information in this book will fit into your own views on behaviour and discipline. Try and keep the information in your mind nevertheless – at a later date you may be surprised to find how well it all fits together!

APPENDIX 2

. . . . .

Help!

WHAT TO DO WHEN ALL ELSE FAILS

Almost every parent has the experience of trying everything to get a child to behave and yet nothing seems to work. Just in case this happens to you, here is a check-list for you to go through to remind you of the more important things to consider when you are wondering what on earth to do next.

THE COMMON CAUSES FOR LACK OF IMPROVEMENT IN BEHAVIOUR

- Does your child really believe that you mean what you say?
- Is your discipline often inconsistent?
- Perhaps your child doesn't know what standard of behaviour you expect?
- Have you given enough praise for good behaviour?
- Could your child be copying the bad behaviour of others in the family?
- Have you given up too quickly or too easily, just for a quiet life?
- Perhaps the bad behaviour has become stuck as a habit and happens automatically without your child even thinking?
- Maybe you have something else on your mind?
- Are you giving enough time and supervision to your child?
- Have you lost your sense of humour?
- Do you think that your approach could have been undermined by someone close to your child?

- Perhaps you have a child with a difficult temperament?
- Is it possible that your child has developed a poor self-image and behaves badly because he or she feels bad?
- Have you considered the possibility that your child could be upset or unsettled by problems at home or at school?
- Could your child be suffering from some kind of illness or are you unwell yourself?

As a rough guide I have listed the causes in order of frequency, with the most frequent cause first. Usually there will be several different causes for your discipline not working, each inter-acting with the other factors to make it quite difficult to tell what is going on.

SOME IDEAS FOR WHAT TO DO IF YOUR DISCIPLINE DOESN'T WORK

In some cases just knowing the cause or causes will be enough to show you what has to be done to put things right, but if you are still stuck, here are some ideas to get you unstuck:

- Remember to use the 6 Cs of good childcare - Constantly Communicate Clearly with Consistency, Conviction and Care.
- Do try to use praise and encouragement and avoid hostile rejection and criticism.
- Have you really tried all of the approaches described in this book and tried each method for at least six weeks?
- Here is a mnemonic to help you remember what to do

P   Persist and don't give in
R   Respond immediately
A   Always be consistent
I   Ignore silly behaviour and praise the good
S   Say your bit - and that should be it!
E   Expect the best always

If you have done all this and you are still stuck, then how about trying the following:

- Ask three good friends for their opinion, but only take notice of what they say if they all agree on what you should do.
- Have a *very* serious talk with your child and the rest of the family all together to explain about the importance of getting on with each other in the family.
- Get everyone together who knows your child well and pool your ideas to agree a plan of action.
- Read this book again!

If things have still not improved at least you know that you have done everything, so don't feel guilty – it only makes things worse. How about taking a break, you probably need a change and a rest by now! There is bound to be someone somewhere who can help you out and look after your child while you have some time for yourself. Finally, do remember those strong feelings of love and joy that you have for your child. It is important to hold on to these positive and creative emotions when the going is tough. They will help to carry you through and protect both you and your child from harm.

'I HAVE DONE EVERYTHING YOU HAVE SUGGESTED – AND MORE – BUT I REALLY CAN'T SORT THINGS OUT ON MY OWN. I THINK I NEED SOME PROFESSIONAL HELP'

It is always difficult to know when it is the right time to get professional help with a family problem and even more difficult to know where to go and whom to ask. Here are some suggestions if you feel you need some outside help:

- a lot will depend on the local services, so the first thing to do is to find out about them. You can do this through your local Library, Social Services Office or the Citizen's Advice Bureau. This will give you a list of agencies who provide help for parents, but it won't tell you how good the services are

- ask other parents and professionals what they know of the local services, but take what they say with a pinch of salt, because individual opinions may be unreliable – one of the best informed people is likely to be your GP
- voluntary groups for parents can be very supportive and give you an idea of how other people have coped, but they don't give professional advice, although they should be able to advise on how to get this type of help
- there is a wide range of professional groups who have specialized training and wide experience with children's emotional and behavioural problems, including the following:

  paediatricians
  some social workers
  health visitors
  educational psychologists
  clinical psychologists
  child psychotherapists
  other child therapists
  some teachers
  children's nurses
  child psychiatrists

The difference between these various professions is confusing to say the least. One way round this problem is to ask your GP to refer you to the local Child Psychiatry Service, where it is usual for some or all of the above professions to work closely together

- don't be put off a referral to the Child Psychiatry Service, if you feel the problem is beyond you.

References

· · · · ·

A. P. Barron and F. Earls, 'The relation of temperament and social factors to behaviour problems in three year old children', *Journal of Child Psychol. Psychiatry* 25 (1984), pp. 23-33.

E. M. Cummings, C. Zahn-Waxler and M. Radke-Yarrow, 'Developmental changes in children's reactions to anger in the home', *Journal of Child Psychol. Psychiatry* 25 (1984), pp. 63-74.

H. C. Dawe, 'An analysis of 200 quarrels of pre-school children', *Child Development* 6 (1934), pp. 139-57.

J. F. Dunn, 'Patterns of early interactions: continuities and consequences', in H. R. Shaffer (ed.), *Studies in Mother-Infant Interactions* (Academic Press, 1977)

J. F. Dunn, C. Kendrick and R. MacNamee, 'The reaction of first-born children to the birth of a sibling: mothers' reports', *Journal of Child Psychol. Psychiatry* 22 (1981), pp. 1-18.

D. M. Galloway, T. Ball, D. Blomfield and R. Boyd, *Schools and Disruptive Pupils* (Longmans, 1982).

J. Golding and D. Rush, 'Temper tantrums and other behaviour problems', in N. R. Butler and J. Golding (eds), *From Birth to Five* (Pergamon Press, 1986).

F. L. Goodenough, 'Anger in your children', *Institute of Child Welfare Monograph Series,* No 9 (University of Minnesota Press, 1931).

P. Graham and M. Rutter, 'Psychiatric disorder in the young adolescent: a follow up study', *Proc. Royal Soc. Medicine* 66 (1973), pp. 1226-29.

P. Graham, M. Rutter and S. George, 'Temperamental characteristics as predictors of behaviour problems in children', *American Journal of Orthopsychiat.* 43 (1973), pp. 328-39.

J. Kelso and M. A. Stewart, 'Factors which predict the persistence of aggressive conduct disorder', *Journal of Child Psychol. Psychiatry* 27 (1986), pp. 77-86.

J. W. MacFarlane, L. Allen and M. P. Honzicc, *A Developmental Study of the*

References

Behaviour Problems of Normal Children Between Twenty-one Months and Fourteen Years (University of California Press, 1954).

R. McGee, S. Williams and P. A. Silva, 'Behavioural and developmental characteristics of aggressive, hyperactive and aggressive-hyperactive boys', *Journal of the American Academy of Child Psychiatry* 23 (1984), pp. 270-79.

A. R. Nicol, C. Willcox and K. Hibbert, 'What sort of children are suspended from school and what can we do for them?', in A. R. Nicol (ed.), *Longitudinal Studies in Child Psychology and Psychiatry* (Wiley, 1985).

D. Olweus, 'Stability of aggressive reaction patterns in males: a review' *Psychological Bulletin* 86 (1979), pp. 852-75.

G. R. Patterson, *Coercive Family Process* (Castelia Publishing, 1982).

D. Reynolds and M. Sullivan, 'The effects of school: A radical faith restated', in B. Gillam (ed.), *Problem Behaviour in the Secondary School* (Croom Helm, 1981).

N. Richman, 'Behaviour problems in preschool children: family and social factors', *British Journal of Psychiatry* 131 (1977), pp. 523-27.

N. Richman, J. Stevenson and P. Graham, *Preschool to School: A Behavioural Study* (Academic Press, 1982).

L. N. Robins, 'Sturdy childhood predictors of adult anti-social behaviour: replications from longitudinal studies', *Psychological Medicine* 8 (1978), pp. 611-22.

M. Rutter, 'Epidemiological-longitudinal approaches to the study of development', in W. A. Collins (ed.), *The Concept of Development* (vol. 15; Lawrence Erlbaum, 1982).

M. Rutter and N. Madge, *Cycles of Disadvantage* (Heinemann, 1976).

M. Rutter, J. Tizard and K. Whitmore (eds), *Education, Health and Behaviour* (Longmans, 1970).

M. Shepherd, B. Oppenheim and S. Mitchell, *Childhood Behaviour and Mental Health* (University of London Press, 1971).

A. Thomas and S. Chess, *Temperament and Development* (Brunner/Mazel, 1977).

S. Wolff, 'Non-delinquent disturbance of conduct', in M. Rutter and L. Hersov (eds), *Child and Adolescent Psychiatry: Modern Approaches* (Blackwell Scientific, 1985).

Further Reading

· · · · ·

Ciba Foundation Symposium 80, *Temperamental Differences in Infants and Young Children* (Pitman, 1982).
A helpful collection of papers presented at a symposium of world authorities on temperament.
S. Gabel (ed.), *Behaviour Problems in Childhood: A Primary Care Approach* (Grune & Stratton,   )
A wide-ranging American medical textbook.
M. Herbert, *Behavioural Treatment of Problem Children: A Practice Manual* (Academic Press and Grune & Stratton, 1981).
A highly technical book on behaviour therapy.
——, *Conduct Disorders of Childhood and Adolescence: A Social Learning Perspective* (Wiley, 2nd edn, 1987).
A very detailed and technical book.
J. Klama (ed.), *Aggression: Conflict in Animals and Humans Reconsidered* (Longmans, 1988).
A thought-provoking work by a number of experts, looking at the nature of anger and aggression.
M. Rutter (ed.), *Scientific Foundations of Developmental Psychiatry* (Heinemann, 1980).
An excellent reference book on the wider aspects of child development.

Index
· · · · ·

Index